PENGUINS

Roger Tory Peterson

PENGUINS

HOUGHTON MIFFLIN COMPANY · *BOSTON* · *1979*

Produced by Jonathan Wrice (Peter) Schults, PHOTO EDITORS, INC.
Designed by Joel Schick
Editorial Consultant: Jane S. Kinne
Production Consultant: Craven Graphics, Inc.
Copy Editor: Beverly Goldberg

Library of Congress Cataloging in Publication Data
Peterson, Roger Tory, date
  Penguins.
  Bibliography: p.
  Includes index.
  1. Penguins. I. Title.
QL696.S473P46   598.4'41   79-10101
ISBN 0-395-27092-8

Printed in the United States of America

M 10 9 8 7 6 5 4 3 2 1

For Ginny

*a penguin addict, whose favorites are
the Macaroni, the Gentoo—and the King.*

Preface

There are 17 kinds of penguins; I have seen and photographed them all in the course of more than a dozen expeditions to the Antarctic and the Subantarctic in as many years. However, not all penguins are found in frigid surroundings; indeed, one, the least numerous, reaches the Equator in the Galápagos, a tropical archipelago that I have visited six times. I agree with George Gaylord Simpson; penguins are habit forming. I am an addict.

My first confrontation with a wild penguin was in December 1960 on the bleak Patagonian coast. Covered from head to tail with viscous brown fuel oil, with no chance of survival, the bird stood disconsolately on a wave-washed rock. It was a Magellanic Penguin, one of the stripe-faced *spheniscid* penguins that are sometimes collectively called "jackass penguins" because of their woebegone braying calls. This one remained silent, attempting to preen its hopelessly glued plumage, a victim of the marine pollution that now claims the lives of millions of seabirds.

I was soon to see many more Magellanic Penguins in happier circumstances, including a million or more in one vast assemblage at Punta Tombo, not many miles south of the Valdez Peninsula in Argentina, where I had seen my first one.

During the course of these austral travels, I exposed tens of thousands of transparencies and negatives of penguins, their environment, and their associates, and it is from these that my editors and I have selected those reproduced in this book. All but seven of the photographs are mine. Those seven are credited in the Photographic Postscript on p. 225). The black-and-white drawings that embellish the text are derived from or inspired by my 35mm transparencies as well as my 16mm film footage, my field notes, my sketches, and my memory. The color portraits in the endpapers first appeared in *Audubon* magazine.

This book, I would make clear, is intended to be primarily a visual presentation—a pictorial essay, if you will. It does not presume to be an academic work, adding new facts to our knowledge of penguins. I leave that to the many scholars who are publishing technical papers, and particularly to those who have contributed to Dr. Bernard Stonehouse's recent work, *The Biology of Penguins*. Among other recent books that you will enjoy are George Gaylord Simpson's *Penguins, Past and Present, Here and There*, which deals in depth with the evolutionary and historical aspects of penguins; Tony Soper and John Sparks's *Penguins*, a good general reference; and Olin Sewall Pettingill's *Another Penguin Summer*, a highly illustrated, readable book about penguins in the Falklands. Further details concerning these and other publications about penguins will be found in an appendix on page 229.

My first exposure to penguins was during an expedition to Patagonia and Tierra del Fuego in 1960 with Dr. Philip Humphrey, then of Yale University. This resulted in the publication in 1970 of *Birds of Isla Grande* (Tierra del Fuego) by the Smithsonian Institution.

In 1965, five years after the Patagonian expedition, the National Science Foundation arranged a sojourn on the Antarctic continent, where I was to assist Dr. William Sladen of Johns Hopkins University with his research on Adélie and Emperor Penguins at Cape Crozier. A secondary reason for my participation in this project (part of Operation Deep Freeze) was to observe the conservation problems involving Antarctic wildlife.

Following our month-long camp-out among the Adélies, I accompanied Dr. Sladen on the *Nella Dan* to Macquarie Island south of Australia at the invitation of the Australian National Antarctic Research Expeditions (ANARE).

Subsequently, my Antarctic trips have been made possible by my good friend Lars-Eric Lindblad of Lindblad Travel, who was the first to take tourists to the frozen continent and whose ice-strengthened vessel, the *Lindblad Explorer,* on which I have acted as guest lecturer, has played such an important role in our knowledge of the distribution of birdlife in the Southern Ocean.

The *Explorer* is a 250-foot, 2,500-ton ship with a cruising speed of 15 knots and a capacity of 92 passengers and about 60 crew members. Besides the lifeboats, there are eight Zodiacs, inflatable rubber landing craft equipped with outboard motors. Although it has all the comforts of a small luxury liner, the *Explorer* is really a floating seminar where the passengers attend daily lectures on seabirds, whales, seals, marine biology, icebergs, and Antarctic exploration.

I also must thank the following organizations and people: the Galápagos Scientific Project, the Canadian Broadcasting Corporation, and the Darwin Research Station for their help while I was in the Galápagos Islands; the South African Division of Sea Fisheries for taking me to Dassen Island, where the Jackass Penguins live; and Francisco Erize and his wife, Julia, with whom I camped for a week among one million Magellanic Penguins at Punta Tombo.

This book was first conceived during conversations with Jane Kinne of Photo Researchers and Peter Schults of Photo Editors, who later examined the thousands of transparencies and negatives in my collection, selecting those from which the final distillation was made. I drew the black-and-white decorations and marginalia after completing the text, which Elaine Giambattista and Charles Schulze typed and retyped several times. For editorial assistance, I again thank Peter Schults and Jane Kinne as well as Austin Olney and James Thompson of Houghton Mifflin Co. Joel Schick designed the finished book.

For the sake of quick reference the names of penguin species—King Penguin, Macaroni Penguin, and so forth—are capitalized but the family, penguins, is not. Inasmuch as this book is primarily about penguins, the common names of other birds, seals, and the like are not capitalized—wandering albatross and crab-eater seal, for example.

Some of the material in Chapter 9, which deals with the interaction of penguins and men, was first presented at a penguin symposium in Baltimore and later published in the *International Zoo Yearbook* for 1978.

Roger Tory Peterson

February 1979

Contents

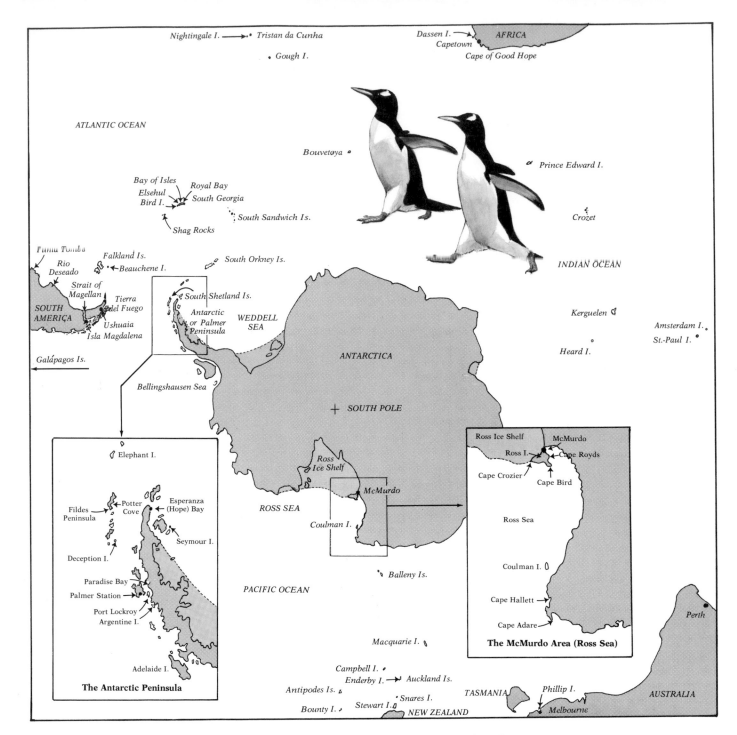

Antarctica and the Subantarctic Islands

The penguins' world. This circumpolar map of Antarctica, the Subantarctic
islands, and the southernmost extremities of the surrounding continents
pinpoints most of the localities mentioned in this book.
The Galápagos Islands, where the northernmost penguins live, are on the Equator,
3000 miles beyond the edge of the map in the direction of the arrow.

(Previous spread) The
Lindblad Explorer at
anchor off Port Lockroy

PENGUINS

CHAPTER 1

What Manner of Birds Are Penguins?

Comical"—"Adorable"—"The little fellow in the dress suit," et cetera. It is tempting to be anthropomorphic about penguins. Using human comparisons, it is easy to think of them as little clowns, the ridiculous dwarfs that enliven the circus, waddling with baggy pants across the arena for our amusement. They are far from that; they are not little people dressed in feathers. They are highly specialized birds dedicated to penguinism, a life molded by the cold impersonal sea, harsh climate, and the crowded colonies in which they reproduce.

The watcher at ship's rail may mistake his first penguins for small porpoises, zipping in and out of the water as they flee from the prow of the ship. Later, as his vessel passes a drifting ice cake, he may spot a gaggle of chubby, erect, black-and-white figures clustered on it.

No other swimming birds have acquired the technique of porpoising, as performed by porpoises and some seals. Arching above the surface of the water and deftly slipping in again, they travel rapidly to and from their fishing grounds. Slow-motion films of the action reveal that their bills are open when they clear the water; obviously, they are taking in air. Long lines of Adélie Penguins stitching the open leads in the pack ice look suggestively like sea serpents as they hurry homeward with craws full of krill.

Underwater, they are as clean-lined as any porpoise. The head is pulled back to the shoulders without a break in contour, and the feet are tucked under the tail, giving further torpedolike streamlining.

Penguins *do* fly, in a sense, but in a medium heavier than air. Flailing flippers driven by powerful pectoral muscles take them through the water efficiently. Some recent authorities have estimated speeds of 15 miles per hour, with bursts of activity up to 30 miles per hour. But such estimates are exaggerations based on the illusion of speed; according to Dr. G. L. Kooyman, a behaviorist, who has researched the matter, there is no hard evidence to support these statements. He reports that when he actually clocked Emperor and Adélie Penguins over a measured course underwater they averaged between four and five miles per hour.

Adélies porpoising

So different are penguins from most other birds that no less an authority than Alexander Wetmore placed them apart in a superorder of their own (Impennes). And it has been argued elegantly by P. R. Lowe, a British paleontologist, that their ancestors never flew, implying a separate line of descent from the reptiles. However, the consensus is that they descended from birds that flew and at some point lost the power of flight, as will be discussed in the next chapter. No other birds are so superbly adapted for an aquatic or submarine life. The water is their element; the air is for the petrels, shearwaters, and albatrosses.

The basic pattern of penguins, dark above and white below, has survival advantages. In the southern oceans, dense with plankton, the water is murky, and a penguin's dark back viewed from above as it slips through the depths is hard to see. Viewed from below, its white underparts all but disappear against the silvery light that filters down from the sky. This natural camouflage, known as "countershading," serves the penguin well when eluding the leopard seal and the sharks. It matters little that this same bicolored pattern is blatantly conspicuous on shore; land-based predators are not usually found on the islands where penguins consort for breeding.

Anatomically, penguins are unique in a number of ways. Their wings have become flippers, stiff, strong, and narrow. The bones in them are flattened but otherwise correspond in arrangement to the bones in the wings of other birds. Some of them are fused or are bound together with tight ligaments, giving the rigidity of paddles. This modification prevents the birds from folding their wings, which must hang stiffly from their sides. The feathers clothing them are so numerous, tiny, and firm that they bear little resemblance to the feathers of other birds. Early travelers debated whether penguins were fish or fowl.

The body feathers, short and rigid with flattened shafts and shiny, slightly bent tips, seem almost like scales. As many as 300 per square inch, they cover every square millimeter of the body except the brood patch. All other birds have bare patches (apteria) between the feather tracts (pterylae); if you have ever plucked a chicken, you may have noticed these areas of skin from which no feathers grow.

The heating and air-conditioning system of a penguin is superb. The innumerable small hard feathers overlap like shingles or tiles to form a shell that effectively shuts out the cold water, which, in the Antarctic, may be nearly 40° Centigrade (72° Fahrenheit) colder than the body of the bird—a man plunging into the same icy water would die within minutes. Beneath their hard armature, the feathers have downy filoplumes, which trap air warmed by the body and hold it there, rather like thermal underwear. For added insulation in cold climates, there are thick subcutaneous pads of fat on the body.

Chinstrap cooling off

But what do penguins do when it is too warm? There are times when even in the Antarctic penguins may suffer from the heat, as on sunny windless days when temperatures are well above the melt point—days when a man may comfortably wear only a light shirt. Penguins ashore may loosen or fluff their feathers to allow warm air trapped close to their bodies to escape, or they may hold their flippers well out from their sides. When they do this, you may notice a pink flush on the underwing, where the capillaries, close to the surface and gorged with blood, are releasing heat.

Baby penguins with their furry coats have another way of remaining comfortable on warm sunny days. They plop down on their bellies and extend their feet behind. While they are thus prostrated, excess heat is radiated from the soles of their feet.

Penguins that live in more temperate climates often have

bare areas around the eyes and at the base of the bill which facilitate heat regulation. They also have fewer, looser feathers, unfeathered tarsi, and less fat on their bodies.

Birds that are airborne, and most are, have bones that are hollow and air filled so as to achieve buoyancy. To penguins, however, lightness is not advantageous, heaviness is an asset. To dive deeper and stay under longer, they need ballast. Their solid bones are an advantage.

Whereas cormorants, loons, grebes, and most other aquatic birds (except the auks and diving petrels) employ their webbed feet for propulsion when they swim underwater, penguins use them only for steering. Assisted by a pointy tail that acts as a rudder, they can change direction in a flash.

Penguins are not bottom feeders but hunt for food where the shoals of plankton and attendant small fish are thickest, from just below the surface down to a depth of 50 or 60 feet. Usually they surface every two or three minutes to breathe, although the Emperor has been clocked at 18 minutes and could probably stay down longer. It also dives to greater depths; a vertical plunge of 875 feet has been recorded at Cape Crozier.

Some penguins feed primarily on fish and squid; others specialize in euphausiids, the shrimplike animals known as krill, the principal food of baleen whales. It is anticipated that the krill-eating penguins, such as the Adélie and the Chinstrap, will increase in the Southern Ocean because more food is available to them; there are fewer whales these days to eat the krill.

A penguin in soft snow can run as fast as a man or faster, and to speed things up while conserving energy, it may toboggan on its belly. Hurrying along with a stride of only six inches is strenuous activity, and an overheated penguin hastening home over the ice will stop periodically and fluff up a bit to allow the excess heat to escape. In the frigid sea, the problem is reversed. By speeding up its activity and zipping through the water at a furious pace, it produces more metabolic heat and thus keeps its body temperature constant.

Because its legs are placed so close to its tail, a penguin is forced to assume an erect posture on land, a doll-like stance. Coming ashore with a bellyful of fish or krill, it may have an almost pearlike shape. Waddling briskly with armlike flippers held well away from its body, it looks, as that well-known penguin-watcher, Olin Sewall Pettingill, Jr., puts it, "like an animated laundry bag."

Penguins may suggest stuffed toys, but they are not meant to be picked up and cuddled; their beaks have cutting edges as sharp as razors, and their flailing flippers can raise welts on unprotected shins. After a summer in an Adélie colony, Pamela Young, a biologist's wife, was so disenchanted by

their aggressive behavior and raucous, yahoo ways, which reminded her of a pack of street-corner delinquents, that she wrote, "I could hardly bear the sight of the little monsters."

It is especially inadvisable to handle penguins of the Jackass group. Their bills have a hook-tipped maxilla that dovetails between sharp double blades. This apparatus is backed by particularly powerful jaw musculature. A Brazilian friend once came on a stray and stranded Magellanic south of Rio and managed to catch it, much to his regret. The outraged bird nipped at his exposed belly, incising a strip of flesh as neatly as with a surgical instrument.

When I first met penguins at home—they were Magellanics sitting at the mouths of their burrows—I wondered why they swung their heads from side to side when I approached. Was this a threat display? Apparently not. The answer lies in their visual apparatus. Penguins have wall-sided heads and cannot direct their eyes forward in binocular vision as we can; they also seem to be nearsighted. By peering first with one eye, then with the other, swinging the head in a swaying, weaving motion, they apparently can judge distance.

Magellanic—a Spheniscus,
or Jackass Penguin

Although the popular concept is that there is just one kind of penguin, stereotyped by the Adélie, there are actually 17 species. These are divided into six genera, easily grouped by their head patterns, as follows:

Jackass or Harlequin Penguins

The first penguins known to men—the early European explorers as well as the aborigines—were the striped penguins of the genus *Spheniscus* (latinized Greek for "little wedge"). Collectively, they might be called "jackass penguins" because of their raucous *hee-haw* braying, but that name is usually applied specifically to the South African species.

There are four species, the Jackass or Black-footed Penguin of Africa and the Magellanic, Peruvian, and Galápagos Penguins of South America. Some taxonomists would contend that these are merely well-marked subspecies representing four discrete populations that should be lumped under a single species.

In appearance, they are all very much alike—piebald, with a white stripe encircling the black cheek and throat, and a black stripe extending in the shape of a horseshoe across the chest and along the flanks. Two species, the Magellanic and Galápagos Penguins have a second dark stripe across the chest. Bare skin, forming pink spectacles around the eyes, aids in heat dispersal when the bird leaves the cold water to rest on the relatively hot shore.

Pygoscelid Penguins

The stereotype penguins, the image of penguindom in most people's minds, belong to the genus *Pygoscelis* (loosely translated from the Greek, it means "rump-legged"). The three species, the Adélie, the Chinstrap, and the Gentoo have long spiky tails and similar body contours but differ greatly in their head patterns. The Adélie has a solid black head and a white eye ring; the Chinstrap, a narrow black line across its white throat; and the Gentoo, a white patch over the eye.

There are places in the vicinity of the Antarctic Peninsula where all three may be found breeding in association. I know one near the Russian and Chilean stations on the Fildes Peninsula. But even there, each has its own discrete enclave within the colony. One cluster of rocks may be populated by Gentoos, another by Chinstraps or Adélies. The late Robert Cushman Murphy summed up the temperaments of the three when their colonies are visited by men: "Gentoos turn tail, Adélies stand their ground, but Chinstraps charge."

The Adélie is confined to an extremely frigid environment around the rim of the Antarctic continent. The Chinstrap breeds mainly on islands in the cold maritime zone between the continent and the convergence, the point where the cold polar waters of the South meet more temperate waters. The Gentoo, on the other hand, is adapted to both temperate and Subantarctic conditions.

Gentoo—a Pygoscelid Penguin

The Crested Penguins

The six crested penguins (Rockhopper, Macaroni, Royal, Erect-crested, Fiordland, and Snares) form the largest genus, *Eudyptes* (Greek for "good diver"). They are all very similar, with wispy golden plumes that lie like wild brows over their red or reddish-brown eyes. Their bills are orange or red, their feet pink.

Some taxonomists recognize only three full species. They lump the Fiordland, Snares, and Erect-crested Penguins as

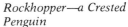

Rockhopper—a Crested Penguin

well-defined races of a single species; this view is not, however, supported by recent studies, which indicate that they have different breeding cycles. Even though they all live within the New Zealand area, hybrids or intergrades are unknown; they are reproductively isolated.

The status of the Macaroni and Royal Penguins is disputed. Although they live on opposite sides of the Subantarctic, some authorities would combine them as black- and white-throated forms of the same species.

One of the peculiar things about the crested penguins as a group is that the first egg of each breeding season is much smaller than the second, is usually lost or ejected, and only one chick is ever raised.

Large Penguins

The biggest and most colorful penguins, the Emperor and the King, belong to the genus *Aptenodytes* ("featherless diver"). They are set quite apart from the others not only by their size (nearly four feet from beak to tail in the Emperor, three feet in the King) but also by their decorative yellow or orangish ear patches. The Emperor, confined to the Antarctic shelf ice during its breeding cycle, lays its single egg in the dead of the Antarctic winter. The King, a bird of muddy Subantarctic islands, also has a curious cycle, managing to raise only two young during a three-year period. Neither make nests; they incubate their single eggs on top of their fleshy feet.

Emperor and King Penguins look much alike, but the larger bird, living in a more frigid climate, has relatively smaller wings, smaller feet, and a shorter bill; these reduced appendages favor the retention of heat.

Yellow-eyed Penguin

The Yellow-eyed Penguin of the New Zealand area has long been a puzzle to taxonomists, who at one time or another have placed it in various other genera. To what other penguins is it most closely related? What should be done with it? To resolve the dilemma, it was finally assigned its own genus, *Megadyptes* (Greek for "large diver"). A feature shared by no other penguin is the catlike, ochre-yellow eye that blends into the yellowish eye stripe.

Little Blue Penguin

The Little Blue (or Fairy) Penguin and the White-flippered Penguin, considered by some authors to be a subspecies of the Little Blue, belong to the genus *Eudyptula* ("good little diver"). These small bluish nocturnal penguins of New Zealand and southern Australia may weigh less than three pounds.

There will be a fuller discussion of each species in Chapter 3, "A Gallery of Penguins."

Left to Right: King, a large Penguin; Yellow-eyed Penguin; Little Blue Penguin

When penguins first met men they trusted them, but that trust was disastrously misplaced. The early explorers and adventurers thought penguins were fit only for the cudgel and the cauldron. When they allowed themselves to be clobbered, they were characterized as "stupid"; and when the abused birds reacted defensively, using their beaks and flippers to good effect, they were regarded as "vicious." Nothing in their millions of years on earth had conditioned penguins to cope with men, and the impact when they eventually met was entirely one-sided.

Birds of a feather flock together; at sea, Gentoos stay with Gentoos, Kings with Kings, and Rockhoppers with Rockhoppers. Swimming swiftly in tight groups, each species exhibits the distinctive behavior of its clan; ordinarily there is no mixing. Penguins undoubtedly recognize their kin by their head markings, and they also reassure one another by cries that indicate, "I am a Gentoo"—or a King, or a Rockhopper, or a whatever. Should a penguin stray or find itself quite alone, it has a loud contact call, a coarse earsplitting *aark* or *kohrk*, that can be heard over the sea for half a mile or more. If other penguins of its kind are within hearing, they respond.

Different species of penguin would not be easily distinguished were it not for their head patterns; indeed, a Field Guide need show no more. They swim low, often with little besides their heads showing above the water, but this is enough to inform a bird that it is in the right company.

Penguins are colonial, especially those in the Antarctic. Some species form aggregations of 1 million or more. One colony of Chinstraps on Zavodovski Island in the South Sandwich group was reported to number 14 million. The more northerly penguins (Galápagos, Peruvian, Fiordland) are the least gregarious; they may nest in rather small groups or even in scattered pairs.

Most penguins lay two eggs, but the two largest penguins, the Emperor and the King, lay but one, which they carry on their feet; two eggs would be an inconvenience for them, if not an impossibility. Once, in a colony on South Georgia, I watched a King try to take over an egg that had been abandoned on the mud. It already had an egg of its own, but it tried for half an hour without success to poke the second egg onto its feet. There simply wasn't room for both.

The Emperor is the most specialized of all, living out its entire life on the sea ice, or near it, and reversing the seasons by laying its egg in the dark of the polar winter, when temperatures may drop to −60° Centigrade (−76° Fahrenheit).

The Emperor, the most truly Antarctic of the family, is the most hefty and may weigh more than 90 pounds. By contrast, two of the most northerly penguins, the Little Blue and the Galápagos, living in sunny subtropical climates, are the smallest, weighing only three and five pounds, respectively.

King Penguins

Emperors tobogganing

There is survival advantage in being larger on the polar ice and smaller in warm regions. A large body retains its heat more efficiently than a smaller one of similar shape because there is less surface area in relation to bulk to release heat into the air.

Although albino penguins occur now and then, I have never seen a pure white one. Several times, I have observed albinistic chicks, both Adélies and Gentoos. Still in their down, they were either pale café au lait or pale silvery, never snow white.

In the colony of Magellanics at Punta Tombo, I photographed a bird that was spotted like a leopard, with white predominating. And twice at Palmer Station, I found black or melanistic Adélies showing only a trace of whitish on the belly. Both were brooding eggs. The most unusual penguin I have seen on our expeditions on the *Explorer* was a melanistic King in the colony at Royal Bay in South Georgia.

Of all the penguins, the Adélie, named by French explorer Dumont d'Urville for his wife, is without a doubt the most numerous. There are enormous colonies of these droll birds around the rim of the Antarctic continent. Edward Wilson, Robert Falcon Scott's right-hand man and naturalist on the

Discovery expeditions to the Antarctic in 1902, stated that there were "some millions" at Cape Adare, where the ship made its first landing on the Antarctic continent. Scott was not the first to land at Cape Adare, having been preceded in 1895 by a Norwegian whaler, Captain Leonard Kristensen, and in 1899 by Carsten E. Borchgrevink, who actually built two huts and wintered with a small party. The naturalist of that group, Hanson, who was on his deathbed as spring approached, expressed the hope that he might live to see the return of the penguins. The first penguin to walk in across the ice was caught and put into his arms before he expired.

Few ships have landed at Cape Adare since. We have stopped twice with the *Explorer*, anchoring our vessel among the stately icebergs and have gone ashore in Zodiacs, inflatable rubber landing craft seating a dozen people. Landing is no mean feat when the waves are breaking against the ice lip. In the words of Wilson:

> Such a sight! There were literally millions of them [penguins]. They covered the plain which was nearly 200 acres in extent, and they covered the slopes of Cape Adare above the plain, to the very top, and they were [over 1000] feet up from the plain. The place was the color of anchovy paste from the excreta of the young penguins. It simply stunk like hell, and the noise was deafening. There was a series of stinking foul stagnant pools, full of green confervae, and the rest of the plain was literally covered with guano. And bang in the center of this horrid place was the camp with its two wooden huts, and a midden heap of refuse all around.

A good description, for this is exactly as we found things some seventy years later. The two huts are still there; one is still quite sound; the other has been reduced by the winters' gales to a pile of boards with penguins raising their families

Adélies bickering

among the rubble. There are probably as many penguins now as there were in Wilson's day. At least half a million certainly—but millions?

The thoughts that go through a penguin's mind are limited, as all birds' minds are, to the essentials; they should not be translated in terms of human psychology. And yet many of the things that go on in a crowded penguin city seem strikingly human. There is constant bickering with neighbors; fights erupt for no apparent reason; and the cacophony of greeting, protest, and challenge is deafening. And yet it is not all chaos; there is a definite pattern of behavior, a social system that I will describe in greater detail later.

Most penguins work hard for the small stones or sticks with which they line their nests, sometimes traveling 100 yards or more for them. While they are on these errands, a neighbor may step over to the building site if no one is on guard and help himself to the hard-earned materials. Young nonbreeders, perhaps two or three years old, roam the colony like hooligans looking for mischief. They are irresistibly attracted to chicks or eggs that have been left momentarily unattended.

There is courtship, as when a pair face each other with beaks lifted high in ecstatic display—and, of course, no privacy when the union is finally consummated. There are tragedy and death, as when a lone penguin, returning from the sea after being badly maimed by a leopard seal, is then killed by a pair of skuas.

A colony is an ancient mortuary. Trampled into the half-frozen soil or imbedded deep within it are the mummified remains and skeletons of penguin chicks—and some adults—that did not survive. Indeed, the colony is built on the bones of its ancestral inhabitants, some of which may have lain interred for centuries, preserved by the polar deep freeze.

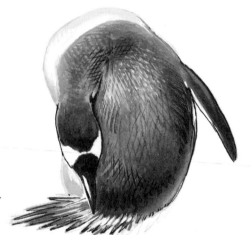

CHAPTER 2

History
and Prehistory

Bird, beast, or fish? The early mariners that sailed around the capes of Africa and South America were not quite sure how to classify these strange animals, which they called *pyncuins, penwings, pinguins,* or *penguins.* Consensus prevailed that they were really birds.

The name penguin, or something like it, was apparently first applied to the flightless great auk of the North Atlantic, which was abundant in Newfoundland prior to 1800 and which had become extinct by 1844, when the last survivors were killed in Iceland. Standing two and a half feet tall, the great auk looked, except for its large flat bill, not unlike a penguin.

The origin of the name "penguin," and just how it came to be transferred from the great auk to the *spheniscidae,* is obscure. I can find no hard evidence to support the statement that it was first used by the Spanish and Portuguese sailors

Great auk

who knew the great auk as *pinguin* because of its fatness *(penguigo)*. A similar derivation from the Latin would be *penguis*.

Nor is it convincing that Breton and Welsh fishermen were the first to coin the name from two old Welsh words, *pen* (white) and *gwyn* (head). Actually, the great auk had a black head, although there was a conspicuous white patch before the eye. It also has been postulated that the name, which was widely used among fishermen, simply came from the English, "pin-wing."

The tough Iberian sailors were the first Europeans to encounter proper penguins when they ventured south along the coast of Africa and rounded its southern cape late in the fifteenth century. It would seem logical that they might apply the name that they had known for the great auk to the erect black-and-white look-alikes that crowded the offshore islands and skerries of South Africa, but there is no evidence that they did so.

Almost certainly, the first European to see a true penguin was Portuguese explorer Bartholomeu Dias, who reached the Cape of Good Hope in 1488. He left no record of his meeting with the penguins, but odds are they porpoised across his bow as he passed, and he must have seen them.

Alvero Vello, who sailed around the Cape of Good Hope with Vasco da Gama in 1497, was the first man to mention penguins, although he did not use that name. After a stop at Seal Island in Mossel Bay, he wrote in his journal: "There are birds as big as ducks, but they cannot fly because they have no feathers on their wings. These birds of whom we killed as many as we chose . . . bray like asses."

This first contact with penguins by Europeans ushered in more than four and a half centuries of persecution and exploitation. As a matter of historical interest, penguins no longer nest on that island in Mossel Bay.

It was about 23 years later that Ferdinand Magellan sailed down the coast of Patagonia and became the first European to see penguins in the New World. They were Magellanic Penguins, very similar to the Jackass Penguins of South Africa, but with a second stripe across their chests. The exact locality where he encountered them on January 27, 1520 has been disputed. The late Robert Cushman Murphy was of the opinion that it was in the Gulf of San Matias. Professor George Gaylord Simpson, the noted paleontologist, argues convincingly that it was in the vicinity of Punta Tombo, where an enormous colony exists to this day.

Pigafetta, the diarist who accompanied Magellan, referred to them as strange "geese," but his description indicated penguins. He apparently was unaware that similar birds had been seen off Africa during the da Gama expedition. It was not until several decades later, however, that they were given a name.

In brief, there seems to be little doubt that the great auk was the first bird to be known as penguin and that the name was transferred late in the sixteenth century to the *spheniscidae* of the Southern Hemisphere.

Of course, one of our hang-ups is to view history in the European context. To be more open-minded, let us admit that men and penguins met long before Dias, da Gama, and Magellan. According to legend, at least 800 years earlier, in the seventh century, a party of Polynesians in one of their great expeditionary canoes reached the frozen ocean that guards Antarctica. They must have encountered penguins and, probably, used them as food.

But penguins had touched the lives of men even before that. The coastal aborigines of South Africa certainly knew the Jackass Penguin, and the Yahgans, Alacalufs, and other Fuegian Indians dined on Magellanic Penguins and their eggs and used their skins for cloaks.

Magellanic Penguins

Indeed, penguins were penguins long before men became men. Like pelicans and cockroaches, they have changed little over the aeons. Man, or a grunting, scratching primate something like man, goes back a mere 2 or 3 million years. By contrast, penguins go back in the fossil record at least 40 million years, to the late Eocene.

There was a time when some penguins were even larger than the largest that exist on earth today. The Emperor Penguin (four feet in length, standing three feet three high) is smaller than the fossil penguin *Pachydyptes ponderosus* of the Lower Miocene. Living nearly 25 million years ago, it stood perhaps five and a half feet tall and may have weighed from 220 to 240 pounds. In the words of Professor George Gaylord Simpson: "In human terms their height would not suffice for basketball, but their weight was about right for American football."

Inasmuch as fossil beds contain primarily the bones of the legs and flippers (metatarsi and humeri) of penguins, not complete skeletons, the probable size and weight of penguins are computed by means of a formula arrived at by study and comparison of available remains with those of living species.

Professor Simpson, using stringent standards, lists a total of 32 known fossil species. The greatest number have been found in New Zealand and in Patagonia, particularly in the provinces of Chubut and Santa Cruz. A few fossils also have been recorded from South Africa and southern Australia. Curiously, the only spot near the Antarctic where fossils of penguins have been discovered is Seymour Island, off the northeast tip of the Antarctic Peninsula. All the localities where fossils have been found are very near coastlines where penguins still live today. Apparently, the family never has existed outside the Southern Hemisphere.

The evidence indicates that penguins may have evolved first in temperate climates, not in the icy conditions of the

Antarctic. Even today, only a minority (four or five of the 17 species) are to be found regularly in the Antarctic. The seas surrounding New Zealand have the richest marine avifauna in the world and may well have been the theater of evolution that witnessed the emergence of the penguins as a unique family of flightless birds.

Penguins quite certainly evolved from flying ancestors. Indeed, some systematists state unequivocally that their nearest relatives among the major orders of birds seem to be the *Procellariiformes*—the petrels and albatrosses. Thus, apparently, penguins and albatrosses came from the same ancestral stock, branching off at least 60 million years ago. Both are superb masters of their environment: one a sailplane that glides on the seawind, the other a submarine swimmer, as swift and maneuverable as any fish or porpoise. However, the fossil record has yet to yield the missing links, the prepenguin ancestors that illustrate the evolution, or phylogeny, of the family from flight to flightlessness.

The flightless birds, which probably descended from birds that once flew, include not only the penguins but also such ponderous terrestrial birds as the ostrich, emu, rhea, and cassowary—the "ratites," large running birds that lack a keeled breastbone, and that fit the ecological niches of grazing animals.

But nearly all the others evolved on small islands where competition was not as keen and where land-based mammal predators were not a threat (until man came). The flightless cormorant of the Galápagos is a good example. On isolated islands, flightlessness may have a selective advantage; birds that do not fly are not likely to be swept away from home base during strong gales. There are several families of birds in which some living members have lost their ability to fly and in which some are nearly flightless; yet others fly well—rails, for example, as well as ducks and grebes.

Flightless cormorant

Archaeopteryx

Going back to the first known bird, or subbird, which dates back to the late Jurassic period, we find that birds branched off from reptilian stock perhaps 150 million years ago, shortly after the first mammals did so. The first fossil of this evolutionary missing link was discovered in 1861 in the Solnhofen slate quarry in Bavaria. It was named *Archaeopteryx*, meaning "ancient wing." Had it not been for the unmistakable imprint of *feathers*, it would have been catalogued as a reptile. Its head was lizardlike, its jaws were toothed, the tail with its movable vertebrae was like that of a reptile, and yet it *had feathers*. Only birds are clothed in feathers; no other living things have them. Here, only two years after publication of *Origin of Species,* was evidence that bolstered Charles Darwin's theory of organic evolution through adaptive radiation. A second fossil of *Archaeopteryx* was found in a nearby Solnhofen quarry in 1877 and a third in 1956.

What color was *Archaeopteryx*? Twice I have painted portraits of this early bird as I imagined it to be. My concept envisaged its reptilian head to have been covered with bluish scales like those of certain lizards. But what color were its feathers? As a primitive bird, it was too low in the evolutionary tree to have developed a gaudy plumage. I conceived it to be dressed in cuckoolike tones of olive-brown, perhaps with a flash of russet in the wings. No one could really challenge my judgment; *Archaeopteryx* flew when there were no human eyes to see it. But did it really fly, or did it merely glide? Its strong legs took it swiftly over the ground, while its clawed wing fingers helped it clamber up rocks and trees from which it could launch itself in brief gliding flight like a flying squirrel.

Birds are "glorified reptiles," claimed Thomas Henry Huxley, the great evolutionist of Darwin's day. They are unique because of the development of feathers, presumably from reptilian scales.

From what manner of reptiles did *Archaeopteryx* and all other birds descend? They were probably crow-sized and able to run rapidly on their strong hind legs. They presumably also had well-developed fore-limbs that, in birds, became wings equipped with feathers.

Birds, mammals, and modern reptiles all descended from a common reptilian stem. The fossil evidence indicates that a new order of reptiles, the therapsids, branched off the main stalk, eventually giving rise to the mammals. At the same time, or soon after, another branch split off from the main reptilian stem; these were the thecodonts, from which both dinosaurs and birds evolved as separate classes. It has been assumed that the dinosaur branch became extinct some 70 million years ago, while the other branch, the birds, persisted to this day.

Not so, according to evidence presented recently by paleontologist Robert T. Bakker. The dinosaurs, the very symbol of extinctness, really never became extinct. The birds, he contends, evolved directly from some of the lesser dinosaurs which, like birds, were apparently warm-blooded. He states unequivocally: "The colorful and successful diversity of the living birds is a continuing expression of basic dinosaur biology."

One offshoot of the early dinosaurs did reach a dead end. The pterosaurs, winged dinosaurlike reptiles that flourished for more than 100 million years until the end of the Cretaceous period, had wings of skin stretched from their tremendously elongated little fingers to their ankles and from ankles to tail. One of them, *Pteranodon*, which soared over Kansas 80 or 90 million years ago, when that prairie region was under the sea, had a wingspan of 27 feet. It probably weighed about 66 pounds, of which 17 pounds (more than one-fourth) were skin. Until recently, this was the largest flying creature known. However, in the early 1970s, three partial skeletons of an even larger pterosaur were found in the Big Bend region of western Texas. Its estimated wingspan is at least 51 feet—the width of a standard sailplane or nearly that of a small commuter plane! The fossils were found in the sediments of a nonmarine environment that existed in the Big Bend 70 to 80 million years ago. This pterosaur probably soared like a gigantic, long-necked, long-winged vulture over the hills and valleys, feeding on the carcasses of dinosaurs and other carrion.

Skin is not as efficient a wing covering as feathers, which can be replaced when torn or worn. This may be one of the reasons why the pterosaurs lost out to the birds in the evolutionary contest for survival.

When the pterosaurs still ruled the skies, during the Cretaceous, a number of primitive waterbirds were also on the scene. In appearance, they were loonlike, grebelike, cormorantlike, and flamingolike. Indeed, they may have been the ancestors of these modern bird families, but nothing really closely related to them exists today. Some, such as the loonlike *Hesperornis*, were flightless. Others, such as *Ichthyornis*, could probably fly as well as any tern.

The evolution of flight can go in either direction. This is demonstrated by modern bird families in which certain members have undoubtedly lost the ability to fly in relatively recent times. In the evolutionary time scale, it surely must take far less time to lose flight than to acquire it.

This brings us back to the penguins, which have been on earth a very long time and which, I believe, share a common ancestry with the albatrosses. Someday, perhaps, if a fossil of a "penguitross" is found, conjecture will be laid to rest.

Chinstrap Penguin

The first penguin known to Europeans—the one that Dias and da Gama saw—was certainly the Jackass or Black-footed Penguin of South Africa. However, it was not until 1758, 270 years after Dias reached the Cape, that it was accorded a scientific description and given a name—*Spheniscus demersus*—by Linnaeus, who was the inventor of the *Systema Naturae*, which gives order to the names of all living things.

The second penguin to be described to the world was the handsome King Penguin, one of several species encountered by Captain James Cook on his second great circumnavigation of the Southern Hemisphere while drawing the "seanoose" around the elusive Antarctic continent. In January 1775, Cook made several landings on South Georgia and was impressed by the large number of King Penguins crowding the beaches. (I landed and photographed King Penguins on these same beaches 200 Januaries later.) During Cook's voyage, his naturalist, Johann Reinhold Forster, collected and made drawings of the King and six other penguins—Magellanic, Gentoo, Chinstrap, Rockhopper, Fiordland, and Blue—and these were all formally described and given scientific names between the years 1778 and 1784.

It was another half century before more penguins were added to the growing list—Peruvian, Macaroni, Adélie, and Yellow-eyed.

In 1835, during the voyage of the *Beagle*, Charles Darwin spent six weeks in the Galápagos Islands, where he gained many of the insights that led to his great concept of organic evolution. He must have seen the Galápagos Penguin, but he did not mention it in his journal; he may have thought it was the same species that he had seen earlier in the voyage off the coasts of Chile and Peru.

The first specimen of this runty penguin, smaller than the others of its genus, was collected in 1851 by Dr. Kinberg, the surgeon of the Swedish frigate *Eugenie*. It was deposited in

26

the Royal Natural History Museum at Stockholm and ignored for 19 years, until a perceptive taxonomist named Sundevall recognized it as different and gave it a name, *Spheniscus mendiculus*. Thus, in 1871, it was the last of the New World penguins to be catalogued.

Three years earlier, a French natural history encyclopedia had stated unequivocally: "Thanks to many descriptive documents furnished by ancient as well as modern navigators, the natural history of penguins may be considered complete." Since that was written, not only was the Galápagos Penguin described and named, but also four more species living on the other side of the world—Emperor, Royal, Erect-crested, and Snares—making the total 17.

King Penguin trying out the water

Adélies in mutual display

The number of scientific papers on penguins has proliferated in recent years thanks to the funds made available by the National Science Foundation of the United States and similar Antarctic programs of half a dozen other countries. Few birds have been studied more intensively than the Adélie Penguin. On the other hand, certain other species are relatively little known, even though their colonies are more accessible. Our knowledge of some penguins is still embryonic.

Ornithology is a latter-day discipline; hence, the long time gap between the discovery of the first penguins and their formal recognition by the world of science. Most of the early explorers were adventurers, traders, and sealers seeking gain in uncharted parts of the world. Their problem was survival, and penguins were to be eaten, not contemplated as one of nature's more extraordinary inventions.

Pigafetta, Magellan's diarist, reported that the flocks were so immense that the whole of their fleet of five ships might have been filled with them. Portuguese, Spanish, Dutch, and

English ships alike dropped anchor at certain well-known penguin rookeries to replenish their larders.

The most historic colony is the one on Isla Magdalena in the Strait of Magellan. It was formerly known as Penguin Island. Ship after ship exploited the birds, which all averred had been put there to insure survival. Today, the island is dominated by a lighthouse that guides ships through the strait. Cruise ships sometimes stop, but to look, not to plunder. On three occasions, I myself have landed on its bouldery beaches to observe the Magellanic Penguins.

Sir Francis Drake, sailing the *Pelican,* stopped there in August 1575 to lay in provisions. He commented: "Such was the infinite resort of these birds to these Islands that in the space of one day we killed no lesse than 3000." When Sir Thomas Cavendish dropped anchor at Isla Magdalena in 1587, he "powdred three tunnes" of penguins.

Seven years later, in 1594, Sir Richard Hawkins left us perhaps the most vivid account of that period:

> The hunting of these penguins was a great recreation to my company and worth the sight, for, in determining to catch them, necessarily was required good store of people, every one with a cudgell in his hand, to compasse them round about, to bring them, as it were, to a Ring; if they chanced to breake out, then was the sport.... Where one goeth, the other followeth, like sheepe after the Bel-weather: but in getting them once within the Ring close together, few escaped, saue such as by chance hid themselves in the borrowes, and ordinarily there was no Droue which yielded vs not a thousand, and more: the manner of killing them which the vsed, beeing in a cluster together, was with their cudgels to knocke them on the head, for though a man gaue them many blowes on the body they dyed not: Besides the flesh bruized is not good to keepe. The massacre ended, presently they cut off their

heads, that they might bleed well. . . . First, we split them and then washed them well in Sea-water, then salted them, hauing laine some six hours in salt, we put them in presse eight hours and the bloud being soaked out, wee salted them againe in our other caske. . . . After this manner they continued good some two moneths, and serued vs in steed of Beefe.

And so it was that the early travelers in the far South knew a lot about penguins, but mostly the culinary aspects—how to kill and prepare them—knowledge that they passed on to others. For more than 300 years, ships' logs were full of references to the slaughter that went on, until, as Robert Cushman Murphy in his *Oceanic Birds of South America* was forced to conclude: "Nowhere are the numbers of the birds what they were before the invasion and spoliation of their kingdom."

Today, penguins are protected (or ignored) in most places where they live, but there are a few islands where the locals still harvest their eggs—near Stanley in the Falklands, Tristan da Cunha, and, until recently, Dassen Island near Cape Town.

The three penguins that suffered most from the lethal impact of man are the King, the Peruvian, and the Jackass. The King is large, and excessively tame, and was particularly vulnerable in its crowded colonies to the depredations of sealers and whalers. Under protection, this most colorful of all the penguins is making a comeback, and a number of colonies now are increasing. They are even beginning to recolonize the Falklands and Heard Island, where they were extirpated.

The Peruvian Penguin may well be the most endangered species. It formerly nested abundantly in burrows in the deep beds of guano—the dried excreta of various seabirds—that covered some of the offshore islands of Peru. But this layer was stripped off for its nitrates, and the penguins now find few places to nest. Adding to their problems, they are taken in the nets of the local fishermen and many drown.

The Jackass Penguin of South Africa is threatened from a different quarter. If one of the giant oil tankers that now round the Cape of Good Hope ever breaks up off the Cape, the entire population of Jackass Penguins, or most of it, will be wiped out.

The picture may be brighter for those penguins that eat krill. It has been postulated that because so few of the big krill-eating whales are left in the Southern Ocean, the *pygoscelid* penguins, particularly the Adélie and the Chinstrap, should increase. There is some recent evidence to support this. But what if krill is harvested intensively for human use?

Persecution and exploitation no longer seriously threaten the survival of penguins; they now enjoy almost universal concern and affection. But their future depends on our stewardship of the oceans. Will we be able to control oil spillage and minimize other forms of marine pollution? And what about overfishing?

Penguins may eventually prove to be a litmus paper of the sea, an indicator of the health of our watery planet. If they fail to survive, by what arrogance do we think we can survive?

Gentoo and chick

A Gentoo Penguin squats on its two eggs at Gonzalez Videla in Paradise Bay. The white cockade over its eye is its badge. The Gentoo is the most widespread of the three Pygoscelis penguins, living on many Subantarctic islands as well as on the Antarctic Peninsula. The other two, the Chinstrap and the Adélie, are more strictly confined to the Antarctic. Penguins of this genus have longer, more pointed tails than the others.

The Chinstrap Penguin, with a narrow black strap securing its black cap, is one of the nattiest looking of all the penguins. Principally a bird of the South American and African sectors of the Antarctic Ocean, it is believed to be increasing and extending its range, possibly because more krill are now available for penguins (baleen whales, now much diminished in numbers, are eating less). I recently spotted a Chinstrap among the Adélies at Cape Royds, the southernmost penguin colony in the Australian quadrant of the Antarctic.

Near the Chilean and Russian stations on the Fildes Peninsula in Antarctica, all three species of Pygoscelis penguins nest within sight of one another, each species coalescing into a discrete group. One rock outcropping may be occupied by Chinstraps, another by Adélies, another by Gentoos. Only at the water's edge do they sometimes meet and mingle.

The Adélie Penguin, named by the French explorer, Dumont d'Urville, after his wife, is the most "penguiny" of all the penguins—"the little chap in the tuxedo"—if we allow ourselves the luxury of being anthropomorphic. Except for the Emperor, it is the most truly Antarctic penguin, confined to the frozen continent and a few islands immediately adjacent. It is readily recognized by the stubby bill and white eye ring. There are many millions of these engaging gnomes in scores of colonies ringing the Antarctic continent, and concentrations of hundreds of thousands are not unusual.

The popular image of a penguin—this species especially—is that of a clown; the seriocomic look belies its true nature, a being that survives under some of the harshest conditions imposed on any wild creature. Its life is hard and earnest, sometimes close to tragedy.

To see an Emperor Penguin (left) against the polar landscape is to glimpse the primeval. There is something so ponderous, so elephantine, so archaic as it shuffles across the sea ice on which it spends its life— few Emperors ever set foot on solid land. Standing four feet tall when its neck is stretched while trumpeting and weighing 60 to 90 pounds, it is the most improbable of all seabirds. No other reverses the seasons, reproducing in the dead of the Antarctic winter; no other is adapted to withstand such bitter cold.

Measuring three feet and weighing 30 to 40 pounds, the King Penguin (above) is second in size only to the Emperor (both belong to the genus Aptenodytes). It is the more vividly colored of the two and has a longer bill. The King lives in crowded colonies on muddy Subantarctic islands where tussock grass often conceals loafing elephant seals.

37

The little Galápagos Penguin (above), living virtually on the Equator, contradicts the popular notion that all penguins are polar. Confined to the Galápagos Islands, it is the world's rarest penguin. It looks like a runt version of the Magellanic Penguin (right), shown with its chicks. Indeed, some systematists would lump the four striped penguins of the genus Spheniscus, regarding them as merely discrete, well-differentiated races of one species. The Galápagos and the Magellanic Penguins have two distinct bands across the breast, the Jackass and the Peruvian one.

South Africa has its own penguin, the Jackass or Black-footed Penguin, which, like the Peruvian Penguin, has a single band across its breast. Many years ago, Cherry Kearton, a British bird photographer, stated that on Dassen Island, where the largest concentration exists, there were 5 million birds, surely a gross exaggeration. There were only a small fraction of that number when I visited Dassen. They have been declining drastically (waste oil at sea?). Recent estimates place the number on that island at 65,000.

The Peruvian Penguin, like its counterpart in South Africa, is a vulnerable species—perhaps endangered. Its problem is the loss of its former nesting sites, the deep beds of guano in which it burrowed to lay its eggs. The remaining population, much scattered, resorts to secluded sea caves. Many are caught and drowned in the nets of fishermen; a few find their way to zoos. Living in the rich seas along the west coast of South America, this species is replaced in southern Chile and Argentina by the Magellanic Penguin.

The Yellow-eyed Penguin (below) is a New Zealand specialty that digs its nesting holes under rocks, logs, and ferns in the scrubby hills or in the forest as much as half a mile from the sea. I took this photograph on Enderby Island in the Aucklands, south of New Zealand. This species also is found on Campbell Island.

The Little Blue, or Fairy, Penguin, resident in Australia and New Zealand, is the smallest of the family, weighing only two to three pounds. I photographed the two birds at right at midnight on Phillip Island near Melbourne, Australia, where hundreds of these bewitching elves put on a nightly show to the delight of penguin-watching tourists, who sit quietly on benches awaiting their arrival. Floodlights play on the water's edge while little groups of birds scramble ashore and toddle across the beach to their nesting burrows in the scrub beyond.

The Macaroni Penguin derives its name from the rakish plumes in its cap (thus "macaroni"—an obsolete word meaning a fashionable fop). In South Georgia, on steep rocky headlands, the Macaroni is the most numerous penguin. Widespread in the Subantarctic islands of the South American and African sectors of the Southern Ocean, it is replaced in the Australian sector by its white-throated counterpart, the Royal Penguin.

Royal Penguins, all 3 million of them, live on only one island, Macquarie, on the Antarctic convergence, 1,000 miles south of Tasmania. It is the only one of the six crested penguins of the genus Eudyptes *with a white throat, its main distinction from its black-throated counterpart on the opposite side of the Subantarctic, the Macaroni. Indeed, some taxonomists lump the two as races of a single species.*

The various crested penguins of the genus Eudyptes seem to have their headquarters in New Zealand waters or in Subantarctic seas nearby. The Erect-crested Penguin (right), with its bushy eyebrows, breeds abundantly on Bounty and Antipodes islands and sparingly on the Aucklands and at Campbell Island. The Snares Island Penguin (lower right) breeds only on the Snares, south of New Zealand, where it forms dense colonies in the scrubby thickets.

The Fiordland Penguin (below) is the only crested penguin that does not nest in the open; it takes shelter in caves and under logs and brush in the forest, possibly because of the annoying sand flies of its New Zealand home. It is confined mostly to the fiord country of the south island of New Zealand. This one, a straggler, on Enderby Island in the Aucklands, was distinguished from the very similar Snares Island Penguin (opposite) by the white flecks on its cheek and the lack of bare skin at the base of the bill—fine points, but diagnostic.

48   *The Rockhopper, with a yellow pompon over each eye, negotiates rocks*
            by leaping, feet together, like a little kangaroo.

CHAPTER 3

A Gallery of Penguins

Although some authorities would put the number of penguins at 18, or as few as 11 or 12, depending on their views as to what constitutes a valid species, I recognize 17. All can be identified by their heads and necks, the parts visible above the waterline when they are swimming. The following "Gallery" offers a capsule introduction to each of the 17 species. There will be more about each one later.

Jackass Penguin   *Spheniscus demersus*

The first penguin known to Europeans was the Jackass or Black-footed Penguin, which has established colonies on 16 islands along 1500 miles of coast in South and Southwest Africa. It is smarter looking and has broader white facial striping than the three South American representatives of this harlequin-patterned genus.

After long years of neglect by avian biologists, the behavior and ecology of this declining species are now being intensively studied.

At the time of my first visit to South Africa, the Division of Sea Fisheries had just acquired a new patrol boat and I was invited by R. W. Rand, the South African biologist, to accompany him on its maiden voyage to Dassen Island, 32 miles north of the Cape Town docks. This sandy island in the cold Benguela Current is the principal metropolis of the Jackass Penguin.

Dassen, dominated by a tall red-and-white lighthouse, is low and windswept, quite barren except for a few scattered bushes. Here the penguins raise two broods a year, laying their two green eggs (occasionally three or four) in shallow burrows in the sandy soil.

Many of the slanting burrows that I examined were occupied, and I walked among them with caution for fear they would collapse. To avoid a sprained ankle or a squashed penguin, I spent most of my time along the shore, watching and photographing flotillas of birds in the translucent blue-green water. Groups of two or three dozen loafed and preened on the low rocks along the edge, while others trudged along well-worn paths to their burrows, where half-grown chicks awaited a feast of pilchards, maasbankers, anchovies, and squid.

I did not find the millions that pioneer bird photographer Cherry Kearton described some 50 years earlier. Today, there are no more than 65,000 on Dassen Island, having been reduced to that low number by commercial egging, competition with the fisheries, and recently oil pollution. This decline is discussed more fully in Chapter 9.

Magellanic Penguin   *Spheniscus magellanicus*

On the other side of the South Atlantic, from the coast of Patagonia and the Falklands around the Horn to southern Chile, lives the Magellanic Penguin. It differs from its African relative in having a second dark band across its chest. By far the most numerous of the four striped penguins, it survived the raids of Ferdinand Magellan, Sir Richard Hawkins, and the countless forgotten mariners who followed in their wake. Although astronomical numbers of eggs and birds were taken to provision sailing ships, this species remained abundant, and it is debatable whether or not there are fewer today than there were formerly.

Not less than 1 million Magellanic Penguins assemble each year for their nuptial rites at Punta Tombo, on the coast of Patagonia. The first time I visited this megacolony, I guessed the population to be perhaps 250,000, a gross underestimate.

I did not appreciate the colony's full extent until December 1974, when I camped there for a week with my friend, Francisco Erize, the Argentine ornithologist, and his bride. Some birds had their burrows as far as three quarters of a mile from the landing beaches. Rheas, crested tinamous, guanacos, cavys, and other endemics of the Patagonian prairie were their neighbors.

I became aware that these engaging birds not only brayed like donkeys, as "jackass" penguins should, but also made a great many other sounds. The mooing, bleating, and cackling outside my tent sounded like a demon's barnyard. From the newly dug burrows around me came not only heartrending, woeful cries but also the most loving of sounds.

One night, a great sandstorm raged outside, and from two in the morning until dawn, I held onto the center pole to keep the tent from blowing away. But the din and activity of my neighbors never ceased. I realized that to know the meaning of the various sounds—to understand their vocabulary—I would have to live among the birds for a long time.

Peruvian Penguin   *Spheniscus humboldti*

The Peruvian or Humboldt Penguin differs from the Magellanic Penguin farther south and the Galápagos Penguin farther north in having only one dark band across its chest, not two. Although the Jackass and the Galápagos Penguins are well separated from the others geographically, the Magellanic and the Peruvian overlap, occupying some of the same islands of southern Chile. It is argued that they cannot be regarded as mere subspecies because they have different breeding periods and remain reproductively discrete. Hybrids or intergrades are unknown.

My first view of Peruvian Penguins was a distant one. I was on the desert coast of northern Chile filming Andean condors when I spotted four seal-like creatures beyond the breaking surf. They arched gracefully out of the water, leaping and disappearing like miniature porpoises. My binoculars brought into focus the distinctive bridled face pattern.

I was not to meet this spheniscid again until several years later, when I spent three or four days on the Chinchas, those teeming bird islands off the coast of Peru where the guano of cormorants, boobies, and pelicans had been harvested for fertilizer since the days of the Incas. During my brief stay, I saw scarcely more than a dozen penguins and none at close range. They seemed extremely shy and, when I showed myself at the top of the cliff, quickly scuttled back into their rocky grottos. Formerly, they nested in large numbers in the Chinchas and in other islands off the Peruvian coast, excavating their burrows in the deep beds of guano.

One still can see a few penguins loitering about rocky headlands along the coast, where they nest precariously in cut banks and sea caves, but they are not nearly as numerous as they were before the islands were stripped of their guano.

Galápagos Penguin   *Spheniscus mendiculus*

The fourth species of this group, the Galápagos Penguin, is an anomaly, actually living out its life on the Equator. Presumably, its ancestors came from the coast of Peru, where its relative, the Peruvian Penguin, still nests in scattered numbers among the guano islands and along the coast. Actually, the northernmost Peruvian Penguins breed on Lobos de Tierra Island, less than 500 miles south of the Equator.

We might imagine a small flotilla of pioneers, perhaps adventurous youngsters, or even a single pair, caught up in the cold Humboldt Current. They swam, with an assist from the strong northward flow, for perhaps several hundred miles. Cruising past the offshore reaches of Ecuador, where the great sea river swings westward, they made a landing on the lava flows of the Galápagos Archipelago—"The Enchanted Isles."

Stranded far from home, but with plenty of fish about, the waifs survived. Through isolation and the evolutionary process, their descendants eventually became smaller and more obscurely marked, recognizably different from their relatives to the south. This species is the runt of the Jackass group, smaller than any other penguin except the Little Blue (or Fairy) Penguin of Australia and New Zealand.

The only puzzle in this convenient picture of their Peruvian origin is that the Galápagos bird looks more like the Magellanic Penguin than its nearby Peruvian neighbor. It has two dark bands across its chest, not one. But then, taxonomic relationships are not always neatly resolved; too many bits of prehistoric information are lacking.

How long ago the first contingent arrived in the Galápagos Islands is anyone's guess: 1000 years? 10,000? 100,000? The islands rose above the sea because of volcanic action in relatively recent times in the geologic sense.

Although penguins may sometimes be seen at scattered points throughout the islands, the breeding range is confined to the westernmost flank of the archipelago—the shores of Fernandina and the west side of Isabela, where the water is coldest. I have frequently seen them on the black lava rocks, preening themselves in the bizarre company of flightless cormorants, marine iguanas, and scarlet crabs. They spend little time ashore except at night, but some, when not at sea fishing, may avoid the hot equatorial sun by seeking shady clefts in the lava flows and dark inlets among the mangroves.

Adélie Penguin   *Pygoscelis adeliae*

The Adélie is the most "penguiny" of the penguins, the stereotype that most people have in mind when they think of these appealing birds—"The little chap in the tuxedo."

As noted earlier, it was named by the French explorer Dumont d'Urville for his wife. Hardly the *bon vivant* of the Antarctic, it has a life-style more rigorous and an environment more demanding than those of any other penguin except the Emperor.

Its identification marks are its solid black head, white eye ring, and stubby bill, feathered at the base.

Innumerable colonies of Adélies rim the Antarctic continent as well as the Antarctic Peninsula and its adjacent islands. I would not hazard a guess as to the total population, but it must certainly be in the high millions. I will have much more to say about Adélies and their colonies in Chapter 5.

Gentoo Penguin   *Pygoscelis papua*

The Gentoo, or "Johnny," as it was once called, is readily identified by the white cockade that adorns its brow. Splashes of color are added by the carrot-red bill and yellow-orange feet. It is the most timid of the three "rump-legged" penguins, not as aggressive as some Adélies and Chinstraps. Why it was given the scientific name *papua* is hard to imagine, for no Gentoos live within 4000 miles of Papua or New Guinea.

The Gentoo is more adaptable to climatic variations than its two congeners, breeding as far north as 52° in the temperate Falklands and as far south as 65° on the frozen Antarctic Peninsula. Whereas colonies in the Falklands are surrounded by lush green meadows and those in South Georgia or Macquarie Island are usually among tussock grass, they are situated on bare stony ground on the Antarctic Peninsula. The southern birds, regarded as a distinct subspecies, have smaller bills, flippers, and feet, probably a heat-conserving adaptation to the colder climate.

Chinstrap Penguin   *Pygoscelis antarctica*

This penguin, with its black cap seemingly held on by a thin black strap, has a dapper, racy look. The only touch of color is the pale pink of its feet. Its slender black bill is not feathered at the base like that of its close relative the Adélie.

The center of distribution of the Chinstrap is the Atlantic sector of the Southern Ocean, but there is some evidence that it may be increasing and expanding its range to the other side of the world's underbelly, possibly because of krill released for their consumption by the overkill of baleen whales. Along with the Adélie and the Emperor, the Chinstrap rates as one of the three exclusively Antarctic penguins. Nearly all of its colonies are on islands south of the convergence. One or two small groups nest on the Antarctic Peninsula itself.

A typical colony of Chinstraps is the one on remote Elephant Island, northeast of the Antarctic Peninsula. Here, where no tourist ship had ever previously landed, the *Explorer* dropped anchor in January 1975. We nosed our Zodiacs into a small cove where we could leap onto the slippery rocks that offered the only possible landing place for us and for the penguins that populated the steep slope. Although these birds had never seen humans before, they were more concerned about the two leopard seals patroling just outside the surf.

In 1915, Sir Ernest Shackleton, on his third South Polar Expedition, left 22 men in this inhospitable place after his ship, the *Endurance,* had been crushed by the ice of the Weddell Sea. While Shackleton and five picked companions rowed and sailed a lifeboat 800 miles to South Georgia for help, his men waited. After several months, all hands were saved. They kept alive during their long ordeal by eating Chinstraps from this very colony that we visited 60 years later. Shackleton forever felt kindly toward these birds.

Rockhopper Penguin   *Eudyptes crestatus*

The smallest of the crested penguins is the Rockhopper, a little gnome with beady red eyes and narrow yellow eyebrows that bristle out into golden plumes at each side of its head. It is also the most widespread penguin, swarming by the millions on both sides of the Southern Hemisphere, mainly on Subantarctic islands north of the convergence.

There is a large colony of Rockhoppers on West Point Island in the Falklands. Crossing the island on foot, I could hear—and smell—the clamorous multitudes long before I could see them. Tens of thousands of the beguiling doll-like birds swarm over the rocky slopes that drop jaggedly into the sea. From my high vantage point, I saw Peale's dolphins playing in the deep blue water below and watched fleets of Rockhoppers zipping among them. Incoming birds swim the final stretch underwater, each one popping like a jack-in-the-box onto a low shelf of rock. Some are washed back into the sea by surging waves, to make another try. Dripping and looking not unlike half-drowned rats, they shake themselves and file up the sloping ledges to their rocky nurseries, where they bounce from boulder to boulder like midgets in a sack race. When the going becomes precarious, they tenaciously dig their sharp beaks and nails into grooves cut in the rock by countless generations of their ancestors.

At first glance, life in the Rockhopper city seems unruly, but undoubtedly, there is a kind of order based on keeping the neighbors in their place. Assembled in their thousands, they jab, jostle, and shove one another. One bird, perhaps taking me to be an oversized penguin, went out of its way to flail my shins with its stiff flippers.

As we watched the scene, a dark hawklike bird swooped in and grabbed a half-grown chick. It was a striated caracara, or "Johnny Rook," one of the world's rarest as well as most southern birds of prey, found only in the Falklands and on islands in the vicinity of Cape Horn. Considering this predation, it is reassuring to see the vast numbers of these spirited little penguins in the Falklands. The population of the colony on Beauchene Island, where we dropped anchor one year, exceeds 2 million.

Macaroni Penguin   *Eudyptes chrysolophus*

The Macaroni takes its name from Italian pasta only indirectly. It is derived from an obsolete usage that, according to my dictionary, means "a fashionable fop." What is the connection? Apparently, in London, some two centuries ago, there was a club of stylish young men who affected Italian ways. British sailors of that day, encountering these penguins with their floppy golden crests, were reminded of the plumed hats and frivolous coiffure of the "Macaronis," as these dandies were derisively called.

The orange-yellow plumes of the Macaroni, starting from a patch on the forehead, are not straight and bristly like those of the Rockhopper but droop loosely about the ears.

Although a few Macaronis may be found among the smaller Rockhoppers in the Falklands or among the Chinstraps on islands such as Elephant Island near the Antarctic Peninsula, they are much more numerous farther east, ranging through the Atlantic and Indian Ocean sectors of the Subantarctic as far as Heard Island. In the Australian sector, the Macaroni is replaced by its white-throated counterpart, the Royal Penguin.

In South Georgia, the Macaroni is the most abundant penguin, populating steep stony slopes facing the open ocean. One such colony is at Elsehul, a deep fiord near the western extremity of the island. Untold thousands of Macaronis occupy a boulder-strewn nursery to which I was able to climb by following their well-worn trails from the sea, pulling myself upward by grabbing the tussock grass. Many of the birds were trumpeting noisily, and some were in ecstatic display, with head and bill stretched forward and flippers waving rhythmically. On the perimeter of the colony, ignoring their rowdy neighbors, albatrosses of three species—black-browed, gray-headed, and light-mantled sooty—sat aloof in dignified silence on their raised platforms of mud and turf.

Royal Penguin   *Eudyptes schlegeli*

On lonely Macquarie Island in the Australian sector of the Subantarctic, lives the Royal Penguin, which some authorities would regard as a white-throated, large-billed race of the Macaroni. All of the Royal Penguins in the world, between 2 million and 3 million, know Macquarie Island as their natal home; they breed nowhere else.

Twenty-one miles long, this island is 1400 miles south of Melbourne, Australia, and 900 miles from the Antarctic continent. Lying just north of the Antarctic convergence, it is the southernmost "green" island in the world. No glaciers crown its summits, and snow, when it falls, does not last long.

The largest concentration of Royals, 500,000 or more, occupy Hurd's Point on the southern tip of the island. There are at least 20 other colonies, but my own visits have been confined to the northernmost one near Nuggets Point, a two-mile walk from the station maintained by the Australian National Antarctic Research Expeditions. There on the broad black beach as many as 100,000 gather to loaf and to socialize among the blubbery masses of elephant seals. Most of these are probably "unemployed" birds, as it takes them at least five or six years to reach sexual maturity; and some may not breed until their tenth or eleventh year.

A shallow brook three to five feet wide descends through dense tussocks of poa in a cleft in the hills. The little stream trickles from a barren place nearly half a mile inland, and there in this very muddy arena at least 100,000 penguins raise their young. Although they lay two eggs, the first egg is either discarded or lost by the time the second, somewhat larger egg, is laid four to six days later.

As I walked this ankle-deep stream, I encountered a constant procession of birds, hundreds of them, some going upstream to feed their chicks, others returning to the sea to make another haul of euphausiid shrimps and cephalopods. There seemed to be no traffic problem—except when I, like a monstrous penguin of some sort, confronted them, disturbing their flow-pattern.

Erect-crested Penguin *Eudyptes sclateri*

This New Zealand specialty is found only on some of its outlying islands—the Bounties, the Antipodes, the Aucklands, and Campbell. This species can erect its short bristly crest by muscular contraction, making it look quite unlike the other crested penguins.

The densest metropolis is in the Bounty Islands, discovered by Captain Bligh and named after his ship. During one of the expeditions of the *Explorer,* several of the more intrepid naturalists aboard made a precarious landing on Bounty. They reported that the squawking and yelling of the birds was earsplitting.

There are always a few Erect-cresteds among the Rockhoppers on Campbell Island, and at least one has been known to stray to Macquarie Island, where, lacking a mate of its own kind, it took up with a Rockhopper. Whether or not anything came of this union of convenience, I do not know.

Fiordland-crested Penguin   *Eudyptes pachyrhynchus*

Although the Fiordland Penguin is seldom seen abroad by day, we managed to spot several from the decks of the ship when we penetrated the deep fiords of New Zealand's South Island. This rather nocturnal penguin is confined mostly to the heavily forested southern and southwestern parts of the island, where they nest among ferny glades, in caves, and in holes under tree roots.

In January 1971, Sir Peter Scott and I were in a Zodiac looking for the rare Auckland teal along the shores of Enderby Island in the Aucklands when we spotted a strange penguin in a small rocky cave. I leaped ashore with my Nikon; Peter stayed in the Zodiac and took out his sketchpad. As we examined the bird at point-blank range, we debated—was it a Snares Penguin or a Fiordland? The two look very much alike. Peter said we would know for sure when we got back to the ship and our reference library. His drawing would tell us. "You will have to wait until you return to Connecticut," he said, "to see your processed photographs."

He was right. His drawing accurately showed the white marks on the cheek and the lack of bare pink skin at the base of the bill. It was a Fiordland Penguin, a straggler far from home.

Snares-crested Penguin   *Eudyptes robustus*

The Snares Islands, off the southern tip of New Zealand, have their own special penguin that looks very much like the Fiordland Penguin, which lives only 80 miles to the north on Stewart Island. One must examine it at close range to note the fleshy pink gape at the base of the bill and the absence of white flecks on the cheeks.

As a precaution against introducing alien plants and animals, the New Zealand government restricts landings on the Snares, and I therefore was compelled to see my first and only Snares Penguins at a distance, from the decks of the ship. Although I could make out a few tiny specks clustered on the rocks at the edge of the green island, and for the record, I documented them with my 1000mm lens, the compact colonies in the clearings among the trees were not visible from the ship. Perhaps there will be another time.

Emperor Penguin   *Aptenodytes forsteri*

My first encounter with Emperor Penguins on the fast shelf
ice at Cape Crozier aroused the same emotion as my first
sight of a herd of African elephants. They seemed too ponderous, too antedeluvian to belong to today's world.

Emperors are much the largest and heaviest of the penguins; they can weigh more than 90 pounds. Broad yellow
patches on each side of the head join a golden wash on the
upper breast. The blue-gray back is sharply separated from
the silvery white underparts by a narrow black border.

The Emperor Penguins—a total population of more than
300,000, in at least 23 known colonies around the rim of the
Antarctic continent—spend their entire lives on or near the
Antarctic ice. The largest concentration, 100,000 on Coulman
Island, was first spotted from the air by Captain Edwin
McDonald, who formerly commanded the U.S. icebreakers in
the Antarctic.

During Scott's Antarctic Expedition of 1910-13, Edward Wilson, the naturalist, made an historic visit to the Emperor colony at Cape Crozier. In the dead of the Antarctic winter, June-July 1911, he and two companions, Apsley Cherry-Garrard and Henry Bowers, made a journey from their base at Cape Evans to Cape Crozier and back for the sole purpose of collecting several viable eggs for scientific examination. Wilson thought that the embryos might reveal clues to the evolution of penguins or possibly the secrets of biological survival in this extreme environment. The Emperor is the only penguin, indeed the only bird in the Antarctic, that reverses the seasons and breeds in winter.

For 19 days, the three men pulled their sledges over the rugged terrain in the endless darkness, facing temperatures that dropped to −40° Fahrenheit and once to −77°. On the return trip, conditions were even worse, and they came to that point of suffering at which they did not really care; they only hoped to die without much pain. Their ordeal is recounted in Cherry-Garrard's book, *The Worst Journey in the World*.

Half a century later, in November and December 1965, I camped with Dr. William Sladen of Johns Hopkins University for nearly a month in a hut at Cape Crozier. The helicopter had whisked me from the base at McMurdo in less than an hour. I felt guilty about that, remembering the suffering of Wilson and his two companions. The rocks they had piled up for shelter were still there on a headland, a reminder that these men were not a myth. Never before had I experienced such isolation.

The great Adélie colony was on the slope below the hut, but the Emperors, although only four or five miles away as the skua flies, were a day's journey on foot roundabout over very treacherous terrain. Twice during the month, the helicopter picked us up and, in a matter of minutes, landed us on the shelf ice within walking distance of the Emperors. We did not land closer because the Antarctic Treaty specifies the minimum landing distance from penguin colonies. Some of the things that we saw as we watched these incredible birds are recounted in Chapter 5.

King Penguin   *Aptenodytes patagonica*

Recently, when I was asked to choose a bird name as my pseudonym, I hesitated. Should it be Wandering Albatross or King Penguin? I finally decided on King Penguin, my favorite species in my favorite family of birds.

The King is the smaller of the two large penguins, weighing 30 to 40 pounds and measuring just over three feet from beak to tail. The Emperor weighs at least twice as much and measures nearly four. The King is less rotund, with a longer beak and longer flippers. In pattern, the two are similar, but the King's blue-gray jacket, yellow chest, and orange collar are deeper in color, more vivid.

Unlike the Emperor, the King is not addicted to the ice. It inhabits the barren muddy flats of Subantarctic islands, assembling in crowded colonies, often at the foot of glaciers, where meltwater reduces the soil to a quagmire.

I have visited the huge rookery of Kings at the Bay of Isles in South Georgia on three different expeditions. Dropping the ship's anchor well offshore, we made our landings in the Zodiacs. Stepping ashore on the long shingle beach we were met each time by small welcoming committees of King Penguins. They stood shoulder to shoulder, looked us over regally, and then solemnly shuffled off.

The main colony is hidden from the sea by a low ridge of sand and tussock, which probably gives some protection during gales. We found no need to disturb the colony to observe it in action. We did not enter the nursery (it was much too filthy anyway), but watched from the rocky slopes that rimmed the colony.

Few other sights in the bird world are as spectacular as a wall-to-wall carpet of Kings. From our vantage point, we could see every bird in the colony, all 10,000 of them. They stood nearly erect, with hunched shoulders, most of them cradling a single large greenish egg atop their fleshy feet, over which bulged a protective apron of warm skin and feathers.

The birds were spaced evenly, each one keeping its neighbor in place by the jab of a beak or the slap of a flipper. Gangs of teddy-bear-like young from an earlier nesting and a few groups of unemployed adults stood idly by. Once, when we returned across the beach, a small delegation accompanied us and one bird even seemed possessed to climb into the Zodiac, but decided against it.

Yellow-eyed Penguin *Megadyptes antipodes*

The Maoris knew this strange pale penguin long before Europeans arrived in New Zealand. They called it "Hoiho." Its amber-yellow eyes blend into a yellowish band that encircles its crown, a unique feature shared by no other penguin.

Although it is confined to the southeastern shores of New Zealand, with outpost colonies in the Aucklands and on Campbell Island, its sexual behavior and population dynamics are better known than those of any other penguin except the Adélie. This is due to the unrelenting drive of one man, Dr. L. E. Richdale, the New Zealander who devoted 18 years of intensive fieldwork to this bird. He visited their various breeding areas on South Island 1378 times, during all seasons, and at all hours. At night, when the birds spend most of the time ashore, he watched their behavior by flashlight. His findings were eventually documented in two highly detailed monographs (see Further Reading about Penguins, p. 229).

When I first saw Yellow-eyed Penguins on a beach near the city of Dunedin, I was struck by their shyness. The moment they spotted me, they fled back into the sea. It is quite likely that the Maoris, during the hundreds of years that they inhabited South Island, New Zealand, conditioned the penguins to be fearful of humans.

It was only by half hiding that I was able to film them as they climbed the dry brush-covered slope to their well-hidden nesting places. Their scattered nest sites are usually under boulders and roots in the shelter of scrub or low forest, sometimes at quite a distance from the sea.

At Enderby Island in the Aucklands, I found Yellow-eyed Penguins not nearly as shy. No indigenous men had ever made them timid.

To reach the beach at Enderby, they must struggle through the matted ribbons of bull kelp and avoid the Hooker's sea lions, which occasionally eat penguins. Introduced European rabbits abound on the island, and some of their burrows may be used by the penguins, but the birds prefer to dig their own in the cool shade of the rata groves.

Little Blue Penguin   *Eudyptula minor*

The smallest penguin, the Little Blue, is readily separated into three of four forms, some darker, some paler, but it is usually regarded as a single species, *Eudyptula minor*. It is the only resident penguin in Australia (where it is often called the Fairy Penguin), living on islands along the southern coasts from Perth to Brisbane except in the Great Bight. It also inhabits the shores of both the North Island and the South Island of New Zealand.

Standing only 15 or 16 inches in its flesh-colored socks and weighing three pounds or less, the Little Blue is probably more maneuverable underwater than its larger relatives. When fishing, it is incredibly swift as it streaks after tiny sprats, herding them into tight shoals from whence it snaps them up right and left. At sea, a high-pitched yapping bark or ducklike quack may call attention to it as it floats buoyantly on the surface. Before submerging, it dips its head as though to check whatever menace may be lurking below; then it dives, to reappear unpredictably some distance away.

Because of predatory birds, such as the large gulls, skuas, harriers, and eagles, these little birds, so defenseless ashore, emerge from the protection of the sea only after dark.

Although in some places, such as Phillip Island near Melbourne, they routinely dispossess shearwaters from their burrows, they are quite capable of digging their own holes if the soil is right. Their scattered burrows may be hundreds of yards, even half a mile or more, from the shore. The colony on the southwestern part of Phillip Island extends for five miles along the dunes and steep vegetated slopes.

Around the Banks Peninsula near Christchurch on South Island, there is a form or race or subspecies of the Little Blue Penguin that often has been given full specific status as the White-flippered Penguin, *Eudyptula albosignata*. It is a bit more robust than the other races and is pale gray rather than deep slate blue. There is a distinctive band of white on *both* edges of the flipper.

While boating in the pleasant blue waters near Christchurch, I failed to see this white-flippered form, but a local ornithologist took me to a small scattered colony. The setting looked like any bluff along the California coast, with masses of ice-plants, portulacas, and other succulent, salt-resistant plants in bloom. Reaching under a rock, he pulled out an adult bird. As soon as we had looked it over, we released it and watched it scuttle back to its dark hiding place.

Icebergs—ice floes, frozen seas. These are associated in most people's minds when they think of penguins. Actually, of the 17 species, only four—the Emperor, Adélie, Chinstrap, and Gentoo—live on the Antarctic continent. The rest inhabit more temperate latitudes, and one actually reaches the Equator. Thus, the penguin environment varies from the eternally frozen slopes and sea ice of Antarctica to such diverse habitats as the tussock-covered hills of Macquarie, the green pastures of the Falklands, the ferny dells of the Aucklands, the heavily forested fiords of New Zealand, the scrub of coastal Australia, and the parched lava flows and cacti of the Galápagos.

Thousands of Adélie Penguins converge on Cape Crozier at the edge of the Ross Sea when the sea ice that rings the Antarctic continent begins to break up in the polar spring.

By mid-November, the great colony, one of the southernmost in the world, may build up to 200,000 birds. The first groups to arrive in October might walk as much as 60 miles across the ice if open water does not allow them access to the rocky slopes they know as home. Although some penguins live in more temperate regions, by far the greatest numbers swarm in the Antarctic, and the Adélie is undoubtedly the most numerous.

At the foot of the icy cliffs at Cape Crozier, there is a constant flow of activity during the nesting season. Adélies come and go, looking for a launching place safe from leopard seals.

In 1965, I spent the month of November at Crozier assisting Dr. William Sladen with his population studies. The male Adélies were already holding territories when I arrived by helicopter from McMurdo. We watched the bouts between competing males, the arrival of the females, the ecstatic courtship, the laying of the eggs, and the departure of the muddy-breasted females for the sea, while their spouses took over incubation for two weeks.

At Hope Bay (or Esperanza as it is called by the Argentines), there is an Adélie colony rivaling in size the one at Cape Crozier. At the far end of this colony, a mile from the Argentine station, there is a favorite launching place for birds leaving the colony, an ice lip from which

they can leap directly into the sea. It is worth the arduous trek over
the slippery guano-covered rocks to reach it; it is quite a show when
hundreds of Adélies gather before there is any great exodus, and then
they literally spill into the water.

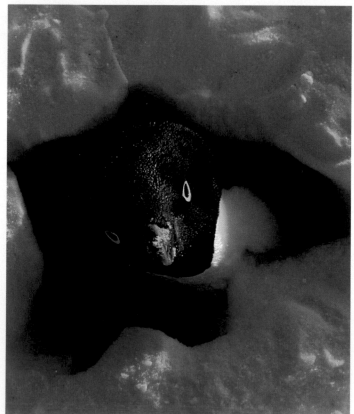

One November day, a blizzard swept down from the slopes of a nearby mountain, half burying the incubating Adélies. Because of their insulation of tight feathers that protects the body from heat loss, the snow collects on their backs without melting. A few birds that had nested in depressions were completely buried.

The Emperor Penguin (right), living on the sea ice by the Ross Ice Shelf, carries its single egg or small chick atop the feet, and during blizzards, the whole colony huddles together with backs to the gale. On fine days, such as this, they seem positively overheated.

A wall-to-wall city of King Penguins. Although the King and the Emperor are closely related (as royalty so often is), they are vastly different in their cycles and environments. Whereas the Emperor is restricted to the Antarctic ice, enduring the most bitter cold of any bird, the King establishes its bases ashore on the less rigorous Subantarctic islands. Its colonies, such as this one in South Georgia, are in flat muddy places, often near melting glaciers, and are extremely filthy. The elegant birds are constantly quarreling, jabbing at their neighbors, keeping one another at the distance that a sharp beak and flailing flippers will allow. Once persecuted, this most colorful of the penguins is now increasing.

On Deception Island (see previous spread), Chinstrap Penguins must battle the surf and run the gauntlet of leopard seals when they leave the wave-washed rocks that guard their colony.

A million Magellanic Penguins (below and opposite) live among the desert scrub at Punta Tombo on the coast of Patagonia. I once camped on this sandy peninsula (with my Argentine friends, Francisco Erize and his bride, Julia). It was not the first time I had put my tent and sleeping bag in a penguin colony, but never before had penguins actually tried to share the tent with me.

The little bays along the shore were protected playgrounds for fleets of penguins. I was tempted to join them but found the water much too cold. The long beaches were strewn with the desiccated remains of other penguins that had died at sea and were washed ashore. A penguin's life is not an easy one.

Magellanic Penguins on Punta Tombo, waddling across the sand to their burrows under the scrub, may be said to inhabit "warrens" rather than colonies. Of the four striped Spheniscus penguins, this is by far the most numerous and, like its congeners, prefers to lay its eggs in holes that it digs in the ground. Penetrating the hard desert crust is not always possible, so many penguins simply lay their eggs under a bush or a branch or a tussock—anything that will shield them against the sandstorms that frequently rage across the Patagonian coast and also protect them from the ever-present, ever-hungry kelp gulls and skuas.

At least 20 other species of birds nest at Punta Tombo. My greatest surprise was to discover a small colony of egrets in a secluded spot among the rocks and scrub—most unlikely associates for penguins!

93

The little Galápagos Penguin (left) is undoubtedly descended from the same ancestral stock as the Peruvian and Magellanic Penguins found farther south. Pioneers riding the Humboldt Current reached this equatorial archipelago long ago, survived, and through isolation and the evolutionary process gave rise to a new, rather runty form of Spheniscus penguin. Its island environment is lava rock, cacti, and mangroves, a far cry from the habitats of other penguins in colder climates.

The Royal Penguins of Macquarie (above) may travel up little streams for as much as half a mile to reach their messy, teeming colonies between the green hills. On these rivulets, hemmed in by luxuriant poa grass and Macquarie cabbage, the flow of traffic is continuous. Files of birds going upstream pass others parading in the opposite direction to the sea, but there is no confusion, no chaos.

(Overleaf) Rockhopper Penguins swarm on the ledges of New Island in the Falklands.

CHAPTER 4

The Penguin Environment

Just what is the penguin environment? I confess that I cannot define it precisely, nor can I suggest a common denominator—other than the obvious fact that penguins are confined to the cooler sea currents of the Southern Hemisphere.

Contrary to popular belief, penguins did not originate among the ice fields of the Antarctic. If we are to accept the evidence of the fossil record, they most likely had their origins in the more temperate zones of the Southern Hemisphere.

As Professor George Gaylord Simpson indicated, many of the penguins that swam in Miocene and late Eocene seas, 25 to 40 million years ago, were much larger than today's penguins. Like the oversized dinosaurs, they died out, apparently leaving no direct descendants. Professor Simpson suggests that they may have become extinct because of the emergence on the evolutionary scene of the pinnipeds—the seals and sea lions—which competed more efficiently for the same food supply. But certain lines of the family did survive. Some pushed southward to occupy the icy Antarctic coasts, while others adapted to subtropical conditions.

Usually, it is assumed that cold or cool water determines the distribution of penguins, and to a certain extent, this is true. Actually, there can be a difference of as much as 28° Centigrade (50° Fahrenheit) between the waters of the Antarctic, where a man overboard would survive only a few minutes and the Galápagos, where he can swim comfortably. Yet there are penguins in both environments. An important factor seems to be the stability of water temperature—sea currents where the annual fluctuation is not too great. Each species has evolved its own thermoregulation to cope with the environment in which it lives.

Today, the Emperor Penguin lives out its life in water that hovers around 0° Centigrade (32° Fahrenheit) or below, and on sea ice where temperatures may descend to −60° Centigrade (−76° Fahrenheit). At the other extreme, the Galápagos Penguin is conditioned to water that varies from 18° to 28° Centigrade (59° to 82° Fahrenheit) and sun-baked shores where they may be exposed to temperatures as high as 40° Centigrade (104° Fahrenheit). No other family of birds has become adjusted to such extremes of temperature.

Consider the air-conditioning problems of any of the *Spheniscus* penguins. Imagine swimming and diving in a well-padded wet suit for hours in chilly water, then leaping ashore on a hot dry beach with the sun beating down. Living in two such disparate environments, penguins must be able to conserve heat and also to release it quickly. We could not do this without the aid of all sorts of temperature-regulating equipment that would, of course, weigh us down and make impossible the athletic activity demanded of a successful penguin.

Spheniscus Penguins have bare skin around the eyes to aid in heat dispersal.

Having spanned the latitudinal distance of the Southern Hemisphere from the limits of open water in the Antarctic to the Equator itself, why have penguins not crossed into the Northern Hemisphere during their 60 million years or more of evolution? Considering their obvious adaptability, what ecological or behavioral barrier has stopped them precisely at the Equator?

The obvious reason, it seems to me, is that being flightless they must ride the ocean currents to colonize new islands and new coasts. The Humboldt Current, flowing northward along the South American coast and then westward as it approaches the Equator, brought penguin pioneers to the Galápagos, but any penguin that ventured even a few miles farther north would have met the Equatorial Countercurrent, which flows in the opposite direction, making further progress northward impossible. They would be swept back toward the tropical shores of South America.

The petrels, which share a common ancestry with the penguins, did not face such a restraint. They had wings and were able to breach the barrier between the hemispheres; hence, we have many tube-noses filling suitable niches in the North Atlantic and North Pacific. One of this numerous order, the fulmar, has extended its dominion to the Arctic ice pack.

But suppose, by some historical circumstance, penguins had managed to reach the northern oceans; would they have flourished? Probably not. Their flightlessness would have worked against them because most northern islands (but not all) are precipitous. Wings would be needed to reach the nesting ledges. But what of the many beaches along the mainland coasts where they could walk ashore and colonize? In such places, they surely would have been wiped out by foxes, wolves, and other land-based mammals, predators that are unknown on the Antarctic continent and on the isolated sea islands of the far South.

Their ecological counterparts, the auks (see Chapter 8), resembling them superficially and pursuing a similar way of life, have filled the penguin niche in the Northern Hemisphere but with the advantage of being able to fly above the waves as well as beneath them.

It is true that the largest of the auks, the great auk, now extinct, was flightless, but it was restricted to a very few low predator-free islands where it could swim ashore, much as a penguin would.

Inasmuch as there are such islands—Funk off Newfoundland, Eldey in Iceland, and a few others—why couldn't penguins be transported there and released? Conservationists would raise a howl if this were seriously suggested. Not only would it serve no useful purpose, it would probably fail anyway because of the presence of masses of preadapted murres, puffins, razorbills, and guillemots.

My friend the late James Fisher, British ornithologist and author, told me of a group of penguins that had been set free in the Lofoten Islands in northern Norway 35 or 40 years ago. These included several Kings, which sparked rumors of great auks. This transplantation (by whom?) came to naught when the birds disappeared one by one, perhaps killed by local fishermen.

The ocean is featureless, and although there is constant movement, one wave is virtually indistinguishable from the next. In this respect, the penguin habitat seems uniform, but as I indicated earlier, there is a great temperature gap between the marine environments of the most southern penguins and the most northern. An Emperor from Cape Crozier in the Antarctic would undoubtedly succumb to heat prostration in the Galápagos, and a Galápagos Penguin, less pro-

Magellanic Penguins

tected by fat and other insulation, would quickly freeze to death at Cape Crozier.

All penguins exploit pastures of the sea that are rich in nutrients. Penguins in the Antarctic and Subantarctic favor krill and cephalopods; those in more northern waters tend more toward a diet of fish.

The lives of sailors at sea—and penguins—are fairly well standardized. Less so are their lives in the home ports. In traveling from metropolis to metropolis in the penguin world, I have been fascinated by the variety, the flexibility, and the opportunism exhibited by this plastic family of birds.

The Emperor, using its own feet in lieu of a nest, is a remarkable example of evolutionary pragmatism. Large penguins did not always inhabit the fast sea ice rimming the Antarctic continent. Was it some genius penguin stranded on the ice that first tried this trick or was the habit developed earlier in places such as the King Penguin favors—muddy areas near glaciers or frozen slopes where meltwater forces them at times to move their eggs.

I often have wondered to what extent penguins of different species, occupying the same islands, compete with one another. Usually, they separate and form discrete colonies or enclaves. On South Georgia, the Kings congregate en masse in flat protected spots often near glaciers, the Gentoos assemble on gentle slopes among the tussock grass, and the Macaronis crowd onto steep rocky screes exposed to the sea.

But in some places, two or more species are forced to mingle or live in close proximity. In the South Orkneys, I could spot Chinstrap aggregations from the ship by the yellowish cast of the excreta that coated the rocks; the adjacent Adélie rook-

101

eries had a pinkish hue. Obviously, this reflected a difference in diet. Another clue: The Adélies spent twice as much time away from home on their feeding forays, presumably traveling much farther to catch their special brand of krill. There was also a difference in the timing of the nesting cycle. The Adélies started earlier in the season and were well established in their nidification by the time the battalions of Chinstraps arrived to find the most convenient sites already occupied. Most of the Chinstraps had to settle for spots higher on the slopes.

The Gentoo, Olin Sewall Pettingill's favorite penguin, is more flexible in its shore requirements. Those living on the islands that fringe the Antarctic continent consort with Adélies and Chinstraps on bare rocky outcrops, where pebbles are the only available nesting materials. Gentoos that reside in the Subantarctic islands of Macquarie and South Georgia occupy slopes dotted with tussock grass, while those in the more temperate Falklands establish their colonies in open sheep meadows, using bits of turf for their nests.

When Walt Disney commissioned Pettingill and his wife, Eleanor, to film penguins for his wildlife series, they chose the Falklands. The reason was twofold; accessibility and the greatest variety of breeding penguins—five species. Macquarie and South Georgia each can claim only four.

If you should ever contemplate a penguin holiday, I would recommend the Falklands—or an Antarctic cruise where you might tally as many as six or seven species of penguins. But if you go to the Falklands, do not make your headquarters in Stanley; there are relatively few penguins within easy reach. The westernmost islands, notably West Point, Carcass, and New Islands, have the bulk of the penguins—hundreds of thousands of them. And it is possible to arrange to stay with the owners of these islands, who from time to time take in penguin watchers.

*Night heron and Gentoo—
neighbors in the
Falklands*

I know one English gentleman—Len Hill—who was so impressed by what he saw of the islands while on a visit that he later bought two of the Jason Islands for a very nominal sum. Because of this impulsive act, he became the first "penguin millionaire," the custodian of 2 million Rockhoppers, 500,000 Gentoos, and an equal number of Magellanics. As a bonus, there were 200,000 black-browed albatrosses.

Skirting the numerous islands and islets by ship, as I have done many times, I realize how difficult it would be to assess with any degree of accuracy the millions of birds in this sea-girt archipelago. The Rockhopper colonies are easily spotted from the sea, great patches of white-washed rocks that are in striking contrast to the surrounding greenery. The Magellanic communities are underground, with only a small percentage of the birds visible, while the Gentoo rookeries are on gentler terrain well back from the ocean. The other two species are but a tiny minority—a very few Macaronis mixed in with the Rockhoppers and several small groups of Kings that are beginning to establish themselves at the edges of Gentoo colonies. Here on these pleasant cool-temperate islands, perhaps we are seeing penguins in climatic conditions similar to those in which their distant ancestors, the proto-penguins, evolved.

Most of the penguins that live in latitudes north of the Falklands have gone underground. When they are ashore, they dig burrows in which to lay their eggs, or they may use ready-made crannies among the rocks or under the roots of trees. This serves the double function of protecting their eggs from predation by gulls and of giving relief from the heat of these warmer latitudes.

The Jackass Penguins that swim in the cold Benguela Current around the Cape of Good Hope burrow in the hard soil of offshore islands to escape the inexorable African sun. Their close relatives on Peru's desert coast choose cut banks and sea caves in which to shun the heat; formerly, they were able

103

to dig into the deep beds of dried guano provided so generously by generations of boobies and guanays—and by themselves. The runt of the genus, the Galápagos Penguin, avoids shore temperatures that may exceed 38° Centigrade (100° Fahrenheit) by hiding in caves and fissures in the lava flows, where red crabs and marine iguanas are their bedfellows.

In contrast to these residents of the dry climates are the ones that tolerate the wet coasts, the Magellanic Penguins that go ashore in the dense forests of Antarctic beech on the rainy, fogbound shores of southern Chile and the Fiordland Penguins of southern New Zealand's humid coastal forests.

Another New Zealand specialty, the strange Yellow-eyed Penguin, also chooses a woodsy habitat, never congregating in any great numbers as so many other penguins do, but preferring a certain amount of privacy, a pair here and a pair there, raising their chicks in secret spots among the ferns, roots, and fallen logs. On Enderby Island in the Aucklands, it seemed so unreal when I entered a shadowy grove of rata trees some distance from the beach and was challenged by a bull Hooker's sea lion while I was looking for penguins. The nests were hard to find in these ferny dells, and the pictures I took had to be exposed with strobe flash.

The Little Blue Penguin of New Zealand and Australia, the smallest of the lot, does not leave the sea until after dark. Its small size would make it vulnerable to diurnal predators if it tried to negotiate the distance to its burrow during the daylight hours.

It would take perhaps 30 Little Blue Penguins to weigh as much as one Emperor, and their life-styles could not be more remote. Although in the popular view penguins are stereotyped, the different species vary in appearance and adaptations far more than cormorants, gulls, albatrosses, or any other family of seabirds, with the possible exception of their Northern Hemisphere counterparts, the auks.

Could volcanos affect the fortunes of penguins? Undoubtedly, there have been increases or declines in some penguin colonies due to climatic factors or the receding of glaciers, but I can find no mention anywhere of the possible effects of volcanic activity—other than the fact that some of the islands where penguins live were created by vulcanism.

The great colony of Chinstraps as well as the few Gentoos and Macaronis that live on Deception Island off the tip of the Antarctic Peninsula owe their existence to volcanic action. This extraordinary island, with one of the best anchorages in the Antarctic, would appear to be a single collapsed volcano. In the center is a vast caldera, or "kettle," ten miles across, which has access to the sea at only one point, called "Neptune's Bellows," through which ships can pass. Some vulcanologists have advanced the theory that Deception may have been created by several adjacent volcanos that eventually coalesced to form an almost completely closed ring. Be that as it may, during the whaling era, when a great many ships found safe harbor in the protected caldera, the volcano was dormant.

But in late 1967, there was a great eruption accompanied by earthquakes. Men who had escaped from the island reported that two days before the eruption, all of the Chinstrap Penguins in the big colony on the outer rim of the island left suddenly for the sea. Had they been warned of impending disaster by preliminary tremors? The colony site itself was not invaded by lava flows or much falling ash, and the birds eventually returned.

But in other places on the island, where thermal water continued to seep from the rocks to form hot pools, many penguins blistered their feet badly, according to British observors who came there after the first eruption to rehabilitate the ruined airstrip. Two years later, after an interim eruption, the seepage in some places along the shore of the caldera was

Chinstraps in mutual display

still hot enough to loosen the rubber patches on our Zodiacs, and I saw Gentoos literally taking steam baths.

One afternoon in May 1968, while I was sitting on the rocks at Tortuga Beach on Isabela Island in the Galápagos, watching penguins, a volcanic vent opened up on the neighboring island of Fernandina, perhaps 20 or 25 miles away. I chanced to look up just as a column of smoke and ash rose from a point high on the southern slope of the volcano. Flames belched forth, and a fiery ribbon rolled down along the skyline. This plume of smoke (or was it steam?) formed its own mushroomlike cloud that spread widely over the mile-high summit as the afternoon wore on. That night, the troubled sky was illuminated a deep red by the fireworks, and we sailed by in the ship to observe the spectacle more closely.

This, it occured to me, may have been the prospect that greeted the first penguin pioneers that landed in the islands. Volcanic eruptions undoubtedly were more frequent in those days, and it is quite possible that many penguins were boiled alive when rivers of molten lava poured into the sea. Compensating for these losses, cooled lava produced new coves and caves in which penguins could seek shelter and find places to nest.

Galápagos Penguin

The Galápagos Penguin owes its continued survival on the Equator to the subtle relationship of the ocean currents that bathe the Galápagos Islands. Its future is precarious, but if it eventually disappears, its extinction probably will not be man's doing.

The ancestors of this species were carried to this archipelago by the cold Humboldt Current, which flows northward along the South American coast and then swings westward into the South Equatorial Current. However, this penguin thrives and breeds on only the two westernmost islands, Isabela and Fernandina, because of the Cromwell Current, which lies beneath the South Equatorial Current. This deep undercurrent is forced upward when it flows against the foundations of these two islands. The upwelling of colder water, bringing nutrients and plankton to the surface, results at times in enormous concentrations of fish. "Feeding frenzies" lasting half an hour or more are frequent, with penguins, shearwaters, boobies, and pelicans all competing for a share of the action.

During May 1969, I saw far more penguins in the islands than I had noted on previous trips, and they were more widely dispersed. I even saw a few individuals at James Island, Duncan, and Baltra. Carl Angermayer, a longtime resident of the islands—often called Mr. Galápagos—remarked that the weather might have had something to do with this dispersal. During the last few years, there had never been a wetter season than 1969 unless it was the spring of 1965, an *El Niño* year, when a slight shift southward of the Equatorial Countercurrent brought more rain than usual to the islands and the sea temperatures were raised by ten degrees or more. These wet years—*El Niño* years—are supposed to be cyclic, occurring one year in about seven, and therefore the heavy rains of 1969 seemed out of phase, a wet year in midcycle. Penguins were scattered widely in 1965, but even more so in 1969. It does not take an ecologist to suspect that any rise in sea temperature might have a direct effect on the food resources of these cold-current birds.

I made several trips in rubber boats from Tortuga Beach to Tagus Cove. The distance cannot be more than two or three miles, but it is impossible to negotiate it on foot along the shore. Steep slopes drop precipitously into the sea, their ragged edges undercut by wind and waves. Here I found a greater concentration of Galápagos Penguins than had been recorded previously in any one place; one day I saw more than 400.

During the midafternoon hours, most of the penguins were in the water, swimming low with not much more than their heads showing and therefore hard to see in the choppy waves; I had to look carefully to be sure not to count swimming iguanas. For every head that emerged on the surface, there were probably two or three penguins below. When I crowded the swimming birds closer to the rocks, they dove, and I could see them zipping about in the jade depths like submarines.

About 100 yards offshore, a mob of Audubon's shearwaters—at least 500—rafted on the water and skittered away at our approach. Among them were scores of penguins, and I concluded that a "feeding frenzy" had been under way.

Prior to that time, most estimates had put the total population of Galápagos Penguins between 1000 and 5000. Judging by sample counts made in that limited area, I am certain that there were many more than that. This was borne out later, when Dee Boersma, a graduate student from Ohio State University, spent more than two years, from 1970 to 1972, intensively studying this neglected species. She concluded that there were possibly 15,000.

Because this species is adapted to two different environments—the cold water where it spends long hours fishing, and the hot parched shore, where it breeds, loafs, and spends the night—its air-conditioning system must function extremely well. This is undoubtedly why it has developed the habit, unusual for a penguin, of molting twice a year, thereby keeping its insulating layer in top condition.

Dee Boersma concluded that this species is an opportunist that has adapted to an unpredictable environment—unpredictable because of the vagaries of the sea currents that in the Galápagos are not too well understood. Whether the Galápagos Penguin survives depends in the long run on the continued upwelling of the Cromwell Current. If it shifts, as currents sometimes do, and shifts so much that it no longer effects the area around the islands, the penguins' food resources will be drastically reduced, and the species may phase out. And there would be nothing we could do about it.

CHAPTER 5

Life in the Colony

A penguin colony invites comparison with a crowded city. The Adélie rookery at Esperanza (Hope Bay), near the tip of the Antarctic Peninsula, has a population of perhaps 200,000 birds, roughly the same as the human population of Mecca, or of Syracuse, New York. The great assemblage of Magellanic Penguins at Punta Tombo on the coast of Patagonia exceeds 1 million, equal to the number of human inhabitants of Baltimore or Brussels. I have spent many intensely active days in both of these megacolonies, but the penguin city I know best is the Adélie metropolis at Cape Crozier in the New Zealand sector of the Antarctic. This colony, by latest figures, numbers somewhat more than 100,000 pairs. If we assume that most couples fledge at least one youngster, the total midsummer population is in the order of 300,000, about that of Rochester, New York.

At the invitation of the National Science Foundation, I spent a month at Cape Crozier in November and December 1965 helping Dr. William Sladen of Johns Hopkins University with his banding studies. I also was asked to observe some of the problems related to wildlife conservation in the Antarctic.

It was early November when the helicopter from McMurdo put me down near the hut on the hill above the penguin colony where I joined Dr. Sladen. He told me that practically all of the males had already arrived, and were holding or disputing territory. The first to come had trudged with short waddling steps across several miles of sea ice to reach the rubble-strewn slopes where they congregated for reproduction. At Cape Crozier, the distance from the open sea is not as great as it is at some other colonies where penguins may be compelled to walk as much as 60 miles to reach home base. A few males, not yet joined by their look-alike mates (or perhaps they were first-time hopefuls), stood erect, with chests out and bills pointed skyward, while they fanned their flippers rhythmically. Their hoarse voices rolled to a resounding *gug-gug-gug-gug-gaaaaa*—their "ecstatic display."

Adélie in ecstatic display

Each day, additional females arrived. Established pairs reaffirmed their devotion by raucous demonstrations. Facing each other, toe to toe, with flippers at their sides, they wagged their uplifted heads to and fro, climaxing the performance with bills pointing to the zenith. This posturing, called "mutual display," was repeated every few minutes. It helps to keep the pair-bond strong, at least for that season.

Dr. Richard Penney, the behaviorist, who marked a large number of birds at Wilkes, found that a majority—about 83 percent of those that had been paired the year before and had survived—resumed marital relations. Returning to the very spot where they had nested before, they instantly recognized each other by voice. Dr. Penney determined this by means of tape recordings. Some whose mates had come to grief during the months at sea were forced to find new partners. A few switched partners, particularly those birds whose nesting attempts the year before had been failures.

110

Based on this evidence, the divorce and remarriage rate of Adélies from year to year is about 17 percent. This is comparable to the divorce rate of Yellow-eyed Penguins, which varies from 13 to 18 percent yearly, as determined by the investigations of Dr. Richdale in New Zealand.

Little Blue Penguins are even less inclined to maintain a lasting bond. On Phillip Island near Melbourne, where 16 new couples were studied one year, 13 switched mates the next. The divorce rate of this sample was 81 percent, about five times that of Adélies, Royals, or Yellow-eyes. I am not using the human yardstick of divorce during a lifetime, but divorce in succeeding years.

In the frozen terrain of Antarctica, devoid of grass and sticks, the only nesting materials available to Adélies are pebbles and small stones. These, the birds gather energetically, often walking 100 yards or more to some spot outside the colony that has not yet been depleted of suitable stones. Selecting one of just the right size, two to three centimeters or about an inch in diameter, the bird trots back to the nest site as fast as its stubby legs will carry it, flippers stiffly outstretched for balance. Laying the treasure at the feet of its loved one, it elicits the noisy mutual display that seems to be de rigueur for the occasion.

Adélie gathering stones

Whereas some individuals work hard and honestly for their stones, others are addicted to stealing. While the homesteader has its back turned, a neighbor may slyly amble over, snatch a pebble, and deposit it in its own nest. Should it be confronted by the owner before it can grab the stone, it may stop in its tracks and look blankly innocent as though to say—"Who, me?" One experimenter who furnished a supply of colored pebbles found that they held a special attraction to pilfering penguins, who eventually distributed them from nest to nest throughout the colony.

A homecoming Adélie trying to make its way through the crowded colony runs the risk of a poke or a jab from every bird within reach. Sometimes a serious fight breaks out, or a less dominant bird is chased and soundly thrashed. At first glance, life in a penguin community would seem to be chaotic, but there is a pattern, a kind of order.

Only a highly specialized ethologist (student of behavior) would attempt to explain the behavior and mannerisms of an Adélie or any other species of penguin. A penguin, on the other hand, must have an innate understanding of the body language of its neighbors. Besides the "ecstatic" and "mutual" displays, all sorts of gestures are meaningful to them. They may bump each other with their chests, chase, peck, and paddle each other with their stiff flippers, actions that obviously are aggressive. But what is meant when they roll their eyes, exposing the whites? What is the message when the bill is pointed into the wingpit, or when they bow to each other, sometimes shallowly, sometimes deeply? What is the meaning of the sideways stare, the pointing posture, the crouching gape, and the fluffed or raised feathers on the crown? Even such ethologists as Sladen, J. Sapin-Jaloustre, Penney, E. B. Spurr, and D. G. Ainley may differ somewhat in their interpretations of these actions. But to be a successful penguin, it is imperative to know this language of recognition, pair-bonding, aggression, appeasement, escape, play, and frustration as well as a number of other things less obvious to the human observer.

Within a matter of days after my arrival at Cape Crozier, the first eggs were laid. On each bed of stones, a chalky greenish-white egg appeared, followed about three days later by a slightly smaller one. Then the males took over the incubation. The temperature had risen above the melt point,

Adélie in "crouching gape"

112

and reddish mud stained the white bellies of the females, who filed down to the sea to renew their depleted energies. During courtship and laying, they had fasted for about three weeks, losing 20 percent of their weight. Many of them showed dirty tread marks on their backs, mementos left by the muddy feet of copulating males.

The traffic of soiled females waddling downhill coalesced into straggling lines. Some birds, in a greater hurry, flopped forward on their bellies and, propelled by flailing feet and flippers, tobogganed speedily down the slopes. Reaching the ice lip, they congregated by the hundreds, awaiting the propitious moment for a mass departure. If leopard seals were patroling offshore, the penguins might wait at the edge of the open water for as much as two days, building up to a concentration of many thousands.

On days when the tides brought the sea ice right up to the shore, they were less hesitant; they ventured forth on foot, forming long black lines across the white ice. Each penguin took its cue from the bird ahead, and when the lead bird stopped, they all stopped to rest or even to sleep a little. Then onward again, perchance in a different direction.

A single penguin starting off briskly on some purposeful penguin errand is almost certain to be joined by another, and another, until a procession is formed. They are so conditioned to following one another that Dr. Bernard Stonehouse, the British spheniscologist, found that he could get them walking around and around a rock, the leader joining the tail of the procession, until after several circuits, they seemed to realize they were going nowhere.

Every penguin colony has one or more staging areas with convenient access to the sea. At Esperanza, the big jumping-off place is at the far end of the long rocky slope on which the birds nest. When their mates relieve them, they pick their way across the snowy drifts and waddle like so many stiff-

Adélie carrying stones

Adélies "taking off"

armed puppets down the little melt stream that cuts the valley, joining others until there is a great parade to the water's edge. There they stand or mill around by the hundreds until the pressure building up from behind makes it imperative for some to leave.

There is no truth to the tale that they deliberately push one of their fellows in to see whether or not it is safe. Just before takeoff, the gabbling among the birds rises to a crescendo. They have reached a decision. In they go, leaping headfirst from the ice shoulder, spilling into the water by the dozens. Incidentally, Rockhoppers do it differently. They jump in feet-first.

Lone Adélies among the ice floes, trying to make contact with the group, have a special note, a loud hoarse *aark* that carries a long distance.

114

Scanning the colony at Cape Crozier, which extends from the exposed ledges above the ice lip almost to the hut, half a mile from the water's edge and several hundred feet above sea level, it is evident that it is not a continuous carpet of birds, but rather a collection of discrete communities, each one occupying an area of exposed rubble swept free of snow by the wind. A few scattered pairs, perhaps latecomers or inexperienced first-time nesters, take possession of less desirable sites around the perimeter, where they run the risk of being covered by drifts. Between these aggregations are broad avenues of snow on which the birds wear icy paths to and from the sea.

I witnessed a late spring blizzard a week after the females had laid their eggs and had made their exodus. The snow-laden winds swept down the slopes of Mount Terror with gale force, confining us to our creaking hut for nearly two days. When the skies cleared, Dr. Sladen and I ventured forth to find that those penguins that had occupied the merest depressions were half buried in the snow or encased almost completely, with naught but their heads or the tips of their bills showing above the crusted surface. None of the males abandoned his charges. I suspect that occasionally the hard-packed snow might become a tomb. However, a male Adélie is able to go without food for as much as five or six weeks, from the time it leaves the sea, makes the trek ashore, takes up territory, mates, and incubates, until its partner, who has been away 14 to 17 days, returns from the sea. During this period, males may lose as much as one-third of their weight, dropping from 12 or 14 pounds to eight or nine.

When the females return for the changeover, they must run the gauntlet of leopard seals, but most of them are experienced at evading this dreaded predator. In ice-free water, they can probably outswim a leopard seal, but when negotiating slush ice, they run a much greater risk.

When the male, famished and emaciated after his six-week fast, goes to sea, he stays away for about 14 days, gorging on krill before returning for a final session on the eggs. Less than a week later, the first egg hatches, then the following day, the second. The blessed event takes place about five weeks after the eggs are laid.

The downy newborn Adélie chick is silvery gray with a dark head. This baby coat is superseded within 10 days by a longer, woollier down. The chick is then dull sooty brown or blackish all over, not nearly as attractive as the bicolored babies of the Chinstrap or the Gentoo.

The chicks are very vulnerable at first, and one parent must act as baby-sitter while the other is fishing for krill. If the temperature drops, the chicks must be brooded. They must be guarded against skuas, kelp gulls, and giant fulmars. Not for a moment can vigilance be relaxed; at Paradise Bay on the Antarctic Peninsula, I saw an opportunistic sheathbill peck the eyes out of a penguin chick when its parent was distracted by a neighbor.

The brooding period in Adélies may last from three weeks to a month; then the fur-coated young, growing fast, start to move around a bit. They join the youngsters of neighboring families until a crèche, or nursery, is formed.

Crèche of Adélie chicks

Why these huddles? Are they formed for mere togetherness, for warmth (as must be the case with Emperors), or are they for mutual protection against predators? The latter offers the most likely advantage.

During this period, both parents may be at sea much of the time trying to satisfy the insatiable appetites of their babies, but usually, one or more guards—"aunties"—are about. It has been suggested that these may not be parents of chicks in the crèche but simply unemployed birds. If a skua hovers overhead looking for the main chance, it is threatened with a lacerating beak.

When an adult returns with a crawful of euphausiids, it does not feed just any chick in the crèche. It finds its own, identifying it by voice. Although one penguin may sound exactly like another to our ears, penguins are as sensitive to nuances of sound between themselves as humans are. Parents undoubtedly learn to know the voices of their progeny during the first few hours of life.

When an adult arrives at the crèche, it sounds off. The chick, recognizing the familiar voice, rushes out and identifies itself (a strange chick would be rebuffed). It then begins to nibble at its parent's bill to stimulate the feeding response. With its own bill wedged crosswise in its parent's, it gobbles up the half-processed krill that the parent regurgitates. After several such feedings, when the supply is gone, the potbellied youngster may still beg frantically for more. This eventually causes the beleaguered Adélie to flee with its bumbling child in hot pursuit, stumbling over rocks and bumping into other penguins. These food chases are as amusing to watch as an old Mack Sennett comedy.

But what of the chick whose parent is killed at sea by a leopard seal, or, worse, has lost both of its parents? While other babies around it are well fed, it grows weaker and weaker. Unable to put up a defense, or perhaps wandering

Adélie chick molting

from the crèche in desperation, it eventually falls prey to the skua or the giant fulmar. These predators are less likely to take healthy, well-guarded chicks.

Mortality is high in Adélie colonies. Eggs and chicks suffer a loss that may vary from 40 to 80 percent. And yet some Adélies manage to raise both of their young. The related Chinstrap, more often than not, succeeds in fledging both of its bicolored chicks.

A visitor to a colony of Adélies in November or December sees them in brightest dress; if he returns toward the end of January or early in February, he finds them quite shabby. The shiny black feathers of the adults have become a dull dirty brown. As the season wanes, the birds go into a "catastrophic" molt, losing the old feathers in great furlike patches as they are pushed out by the new plumage beneath. Most Adélies prefer to go through this difficult two-week period on the offshore ice floes, but all adult Chinstraps seem to complete the molt in or near the colony.

The young birds are seven to eight weeks old when they lose their baby fluff. Now left largely to their own devices, they are a comical, disreputable-looking crowd with tufts of brown wool half concealing their shiny new undergarments. When the molt is complete, they have a waterproof swimsuit and can enter the sea.

At Hallett Station, I once saw thousands of young in this transitional state. Ten days later, when our ship returned, all but a few had gone. There had been a mass exodus; only a few young and almost no adults were present. Most of these late chicks, unguarded and neglected, would probably succumb to the skuas. It was questionable whether or not more than 5 percent of them would survive.

In describing the life of the colony, I have chosen the Adélie as the stereotype penguin. Certainly, it is the best known, even though its environment is far harsher than that endured by any other penguin except the Emperor. Because it exists in such large numbers in a relatively simplified ecosystem, it is attractive to investigators, who can more readily analyze population dynamics and behavior patterns (but one must not forget all those research grants for Antarctic studies and the amenities that are provided).

The life patterns of the other two *pygoscelid* penguins, the Chinstrap and the Gentoo, are similar to those of the Adélie, differing only in details. In the South Shetlands, where the three nest near one another I have been able to sit in one place to compare the similarities and the subtle differences.

At Signy Island in the South Orkneys, where Chinstraps and Adélies have been studied comparatively by members of the British Antarctic Survey, Chinstraps start to breed three weeks later than Adélies and therefore are forced to use the higher, rockier slopes. In spite of this seeming disadvantage, Chinstraps were found to be away from the nest for shorter periods and raised their young faster, suggesting that they did not have to travel as far offshore to reach their feeding grounds.

The Gentoo is more flexible in its way of life than the Adélie and the Chinstrap. On the Antarctic Peninsula and its nearby islands, it shares the same rocky nesting sites, the same harsh climate, the same predators with the other two; in the Falklands, it enjoys a milder climate, makes its nest of grass and turf, and has a different set of bird neighbors and predators. In the Antarctic, it may not lay its eggs until December or early January, whereas in the Falklands it is able to start three months earlier.

We can make some generalizations about penguin colonies. Those in the Antarctic and the Subantarctic—such as the colonies of Adélies, Chinstraps, Kings, and Macaronis—are the largest, most crowded, and most exposed to the elements. The penguins that live farthest north in subtropical or tropical latitudes—such as the Fiordland, Yellow-eyed, Little Blue, Peruvian, and Galápagos—tend to be less gregarious. Their colonies usually have a looser structure, and the nests are hidden in burrows or under rocks.

The four jackass, or harlequin, penguins all nest underground, under bushes, or at least with some protection from the sun. They may congregate in immense numbers, a million or more, as Magellanics do at Punta Tombo in Patagonia and as African Jackass Penguins formerly did at Dassen Island near Cape Town. Or they may nest in very small scattered groups or even in single pairs as they do in some places along the coasts of Chile and Peru and in the Galápagos. By nesting in their little caves and under the bushes, they are relatively secure from harassment by gulls and skuas. At Punta Tombo, those resourceful predators find easier pickings among the masses of phlegmatic cormorants (three species) that reside near the rocky tip of the point.

The ground in which Magellanics dig their burrows is like an ancient graveyard. The fragmentary remains of hundreds of generations are buried deep under the pebbles, earth, and drifting sand. Some colony sites almost certainly go back thousands of years and can claim a greater antiquity, a longer history of occupancy than any human city.

Late each day, tens of thousands of penguins mass on the pebbly beaches of Punta Tombo in what appear to be social gatherings. Inasmuch as these Magellanics live on a peninsula of the mainland where foxes roam, they are not as trusting as some of the other penguins—Adélies, for example—which are not threatened by land-based mammals.

At Punta Tombo, I was definitely an intruder, and when I walked down the beach toward the birds, they moved away in a mass. However, in the rock-rimmed coves where large parties bathed and played water games, they eventually accepted me as part of the scenery. If I sat still for a while, they would even tug at my boots and my camera equipment.

The crested penguins, more than any other group, are pure fun. I remember a magic day on the beach at Royal Bay in South Georgia with Macaroni Penguins swarming around us, squabbling, playing in the surf, bathing, making love. It was an elfin world. While one bird was busily preening, my wife, Virginia, stroked it gently and held its extended flipper. The bird kept on preening, completely accepting the familiarity.

Not all crested penguins are as delightfully friendly as some Macaronis and Royals. Rockhoppers can be especially feisty. In general, there seems to be more going on in a colony of *Eudyptes* penguins, more exaggerated displays, more trumpeting, more bowing and head weaving—and far more scrapping and turmoil.

One very functional bit of body language has been called the "slender walk." When a bird wants to make its way through the crowd without being assaulted, it sleeks its feathers, lowers its head, and holds its flippers stiffly forward. This presumably means to other penguins, "Let me through; no fights, please."

One of the curious things about the crested penguins is that the first egg is much smaller than the second. This has nothing to do with its viability, but it is usually ejected (probably not deliberately) or is lost before the second is laid, probably because of the incessant squabbles of pugnacious males. If both eggs hatch, as they sometimes do, only one chick survives the first few days. There is no evidence, according to Dr. John Warham of Canterbury University, that a second is ever successfully raised, although he records one instance where the second chick of a Fiordland Penguin survived at least 19 days.

Of all penguins, the Little Blue of Australia and New Zealand is the one that lives in closest association with men. On my first visit to Phillip Island near Melbourne with an Australian friend, Graham Pizzey, we spent the night in a summer cottage where penguins were all around. Fortunately for my eardrums, they were not under the bedroom window or beneath the floorboards as they are in some houses along the coast. Here most of them were nesting in association with short-tailed shearwaters, or "mutton-birds," whose burrows peppered the turf like rabbit warrens. The darkness resounded with mewing notes, screams, gargles, growls, and hoarse trumpetings. They brayed not unlike Jackass Penguins, inhaling and exhaling asthmatically until they reached a frenzy of sound. All this cacophony, mingling with the hysterical *koo-roo-ah* of the shearwaters, conjured up visions of banshees in torment. When we threw the beams of our flashlights on the birds, their normal behavior became inhibited; they fell silent and scuttled into their burrows.

In the fenced-off reserve at nearby Summerlands, which is partly illuminated by floodlights, their behavior can be more readily observed. When a mate comes home from the sea, the one who remained emerges from the burrow, and they greet

122

each other with ceremonial gestures and much raucous braying. Graham Pizzey commented that the effect, when several hundred reunions are taking place, is like hundreds of small, rather demented jackasses braying in antiphony.

An enthusiastic group of amateur ornithologists organized by Peter Balmford and Pauline Reilly spent four seasons with the penguins in the reserve at Summerlands and were able to tell us many things about the breeding success of this colony. Of the eggs laid during a four-year period, only two out of five resulted in fledged chicks. It was learned that two clutches of two eggs each were often laid in a single season and that some pairs were able to raise at least one chick both times. Occasionally, after two failures a pair may even try a third time in the same year—again without success. Are they born losers?

Emperor cradling its chick

The two largest penguins, the Emperor and the King, are the least like the others, each having a life pattern unique among birds. As noted before, the imposing Emperor is the most improbable of all, reversing the seasons by breeding during the long night of the Antarctic winter. It is the only bird in the world that may live out its life without touching land. Most of its two dozen known colonies are on shelf ice, which goes out with the spring thaws; only two are on beaches.

Few men have ever seen an Emperor on its egg because most biologists are in the Antarctic only during the summer months, when the entire population of these birds is somewhere out in the open pack ice. Just where most of them are is a puzzle. I have seen very few at sea during my dozen expeditions to the Antarctic.

In March or April (equivalent to September or October in the North), after the Adélies have abandoned their own col-

A crèche of baby Emperors

onies around the rim of the Antarctic continent and have moved north into the pack ice, the Emperors start south. Having consumed vast quantities of fish, squid, and shrimp they are at maximum weight, which will enable them to live off their fat for many weeks. Majestically, they march homeward in long lines across the polar ice. The impressive processions of giants plod solemnly for miles, impelled by their genes to reproduce and to survive in the most inhospitable bird environment in the world.

Emperor chick

When the multitude has assembled in their Mecca, usually in the lee of an ice cliff, an island, or a coastal hill, they may number many thousands. For the next two months, there is a great deal of socializing, sorting themselves out, reuniting with former mates, or making new alliances.

The large golden patches on their necks must have some significance because the pairs indulge in displays or advertising walks, swinging the head from side to side as they promenade, exhibiting one yellow patch and then the other. Certainly, there must be some color perception in penguins; why else these patches? Or why the colorful bills, feet, or crests in some of the other species?

The musical trumpetings of Emperors and Kings are quite unlike the raucous calls of other penguins. The "song," if we may call it that, is delivered by the pair in duet, with heads dipped low against their chests and bills pointed down. In mutual display, they face each other, and after dipping their heads in song, they raise them high while slowly waving their flippers.

As the hours of daylight become shorter and the bitter winds of winter begin to sweep down from the Antarctic ice cap, the Emperors form great huddles not unlike the crèche assemblies that the chicks will form later. They are much more tolerant of crowding than other penguins; it is essential for their comfort and survival.

The rough-shelled greenish-white egg appears in May or June, which is early winter in the Antarctic. Immediately after it is laid, the female, who has lost 20 percent of her weight during courtship and laying, returns to the sea. She leaves the task of incubation to the male, and to keep the pear-shaped egg off the ice, he places it on his feet, deftly tucking it close to his body under a warm muff of belly skin. When bored with standing or half squatting in one spot, he can actually shuffle about with the egg. For 60 to 65 days—

125

during two full months of continuous darkness, when temperatures may drop to $-51°$ or $-57°$ Centigrade ($-60°$ or $-70°$ Fahrenheit)—he plays nursemaid to that egg, and by the time his mate has returned with a full belly, his own weight has gone down by 30 to 45 percent—during the four months without food, he may drop from 90 pounds to 50 pounds.

Usually, the baby hatches just before the female returns, and it is the male who gives the newborn its first meal, a nourishing secretion from his esophagus that tides the infant over those first uncertain days.

Although King and Emperor Penguins are closely related and look much alike, their young are very dissimilar. Young Kings are nearly naked when they hatch but soon acquire an unkempt woolly brown coat. Young Emperors start life a bit more clothed and are much more attractive, pearly gray with a white face framed in a black cap and black earmuffs. This contrasting head pattern peeping from above the parental feet may be visually helpful at feeding time in the polar night.

So strong is the urge to mother something, that no egg or chick goes long unattended. An egg that is addled and frozen may be picked up by an unemployed bird and tucked under the fur muff that covers its feet; lacking an egg, a piece of ice of the right size and shape may do as well, or even a long-dead chick. There is undoubtedly survival value in this insatiable drive, a sort of instinctive altruism. When an egg or small chick is dropped momentarily, it is adopted by a neighbor. There may be a scrimmage involving several unoccupied adults, during which the chick may suffer injury; or it may scramble away from the brawl to be snatched up by someone else, perhaps its rightful parent. It may fall into a crevice, never to be retrieved. In balance, however, Emperors succeed in raising a greater percentage of their chicks than most other penguins.

At the time of my second visit to the Emperors at Cape

A pair of King Penguins about to transfer their egg

Crozier in 1965, two of Dr. Sladen's associates, John Boyd and Jeff Harrow, were camping near the colony. They herded the crèches into improvised pens where the chicks, now very large, were weighed, examined, and fitted with plastic flipper bands. It was December, and within a month they would be going into molt, exchanging their fuzzy gray baby coats for hard juvenile plumage. If the sea ice broke away from the Ross Ice Shelf before the molt was completed, as it often did, they would float away on rafts of ice until they were ready to take up life in the water at the age of five to five and a half months. Then they would look rather like their parents, but less colorful. In another 18 months, after molting again, they would be virtually indistinguishable from the adults, but most of them would not breed until they were at least six years old.

The muddy nurseries of the King Penguin on the Subantarctic islands are quite unlike the icy ones of the Emperor on the rim of the Antarctic continent. Like the Emperors, each incubating bird holds a single rough greenish-white egg on its feet, but the birds are evenly spaced, each keeping its neighbor in place with jabs of the beak and flailing flippers. They obviously are less tolerant of crowding than Emperors. Living in a less extreme environment and incubating in summer rather than in midwinter, they do not need cheek-to-jowl togetherness.

When a bird returns to relieve its mate of the pear-shaped egg, there is a mutual display of head waving, nibbling, and fencing with head and neck; this is accompanied by musical trumpeting. Sometimes an unfortunate bird that does not observe the right behavioral signals as it proceeds through the colony is assailed from all sides until a free-for-all develops. The silvery breasts of combatants are sometimes bloodied by the bruising flippers of their opponents. My wife, Ginny, observing this seeming mayhem for the first time, was dismayed. She commented: "They aren't very nice to each other, are they?"

In muddy swales at the edge of the main colony, large gangs of adolescent chicks swathed in brown fur muffs loaf listlessly. These are last year's chicks; soon they will molt and enter the sea, looking somewhat like their parents, but less colorful. Inasmuch as it may take a chick up to 13 months to fledge (more than twice as long as it takes a young Emperor), reproduction in King Penguins is on a unique cycle. A pair can successfully raise only two young during a three-year period. In the third year, laying is so late that eggs or chicks do not survive the rigors of winter.

Each species of penguin would seem to have limited options and a locked-in rigidity of behavior, but as a family, these unbirdlike birds, interacting with their environment, have shown remarkable flexibility.

Young King molting

A pair of Magellanic Penguins in the huge colony at Punta Tombo.

Penguins greet one another at the nest with much ceremony. Standing chest to chest, with bills pointed upward, they wag their heads from side to side as though they were earnestly confirming their commitment to each other. The pair of Chinstrap Penguins (left, above) and the pair of Adélies (right, above) are engaged in this kind of display, which helps keep the pair bond strong. Males in the heat of courtship also have what has been called an "ecstatic display." With the bill raised to the zenith, they wave their flippers rhythmically.

The Rockhopper (above) and Magellanic Penguins (opposite page below) are indulging in less intensive conjugal activities. Simply affection, perhaps? The fondling and nuzzling that all lovers enjoy? It is difficult not to be anthropomorphic about many of the things that penguins do.

(Previous spread) When I investigated this devoted couple, they turned their heads from side to side, peering at me first with one eye, then the other, as though to establish distance. Convinced that I was up to no good, they threatened me with open mouths and brayed like jackasses.

Most penguins lay two eggs, except for the King (upper left) and the Emperor, both of which lay single eggs that they carry on top of their feet, tucked beneath a loose warm apron of belly feathers.

During unseasonable blizzards in December, snow may cover the incubating Adélies. I have seen birds so crusted over that only their heads or the tips of their beaks showed. The perplexed Adélie to the left, perhaps an inexperienced bird, elected to lay its eggs in a low spot. Established pairs usually command windswept, snow-free rises of ground.

Whereas it may take nine weeks for the egg of an Emperor Penguin to hatch, and seven and a half weeks for that of a King, the Gentoo Penguin (lower left and right) hatches in five to five and a half weeks.

An elegant Chinstrap Penguin (above) feeds its two silvery gray chicks. The baby on the left is positively potbellied from the amount of krill that has been pumped into it and thus is no longer interested in food. Now it is the other chick's turn. Pecking at its parent's bill, it stimulates the feeding reaction. No time is wasted when regurgitation starts; thrusting its head deep into the open mouth, it will soon become as bulbous as its twin.

The Magellanic Penguin (right) feeds its young by regurgitation in much the same manner. Not a scrap of food is lost unless a dolphin gull interferes, causing the bird to spill its hard-earned catch of squid or fish. While one parent is feeding or guarding the babies, the other may be out fishing. Meals become less frequent as the weeks go on, eventually forcing the fully grown youngster to take to the sea and fend for itself.

The Gentoo Penguin (right) may take care of its two pretty babies at the nest site for as much as five or six weeks before they join the crèches. Then the little gangs of young are guarded by a solicitous "auntie" or two who fend off the skuas and other dangers while parents are away filling the market basket. When they are three months old, or perhaps a bit younger, the well-grown youngsters wander down to the sea to shift for themselves.

King Penguins (below) have a much longer babyhood. They are nine or ten months old before they shed their brown teddy-bear coats. However, they must endure the winter in the colony and be fed again in the spring before they can leave for the sea, as many as 13 months after hatching.

A wandering young Adélie Penguin that does not quickly join a crèche is in for trouble. The skua, a gull-like bird with hawklike instincts, is a constant threat. Whereas an adult Adélie, such as the one above, is fully capable of dealing with a skua, the fat and inexperienced young birds are not. Hovering above the little crèche, looking for a weakling

or a stray, the skua is usually thwarted and must go hungry. It is not easy to be a predator. Skuas usually are more successful when two or more work as a team. Every crèche of Adélies has at least one "auntie" on guard, or there may be as many as half a dozen, which courageously defend their helpless charges.

In many penguin colonies, skuas (below) are not only predators that eat eggs, chicks, and disabled adults, but they also are scavengers, cleaning up the remains of penguins that have died. They also may pick at the bits and pieces clinging to a carcass after a leopard seal has made its kill.

The sheathbill (upper right), a scavenger with the look of a white pigeon, prowls about looking for a chance to steal an unguarded egg. When a penguin comes in with a crawful of krill to feed its young, this aggressive scrounger may interfere and force the bird to spill the food on the ground.

In the Falklands, the "Johnny Rook" or Austral caracara (below),
a kind of hawk, snatches chicks from the midst of Rockhopper colonies. But so multitudinous are the penguins that the effect of this
predation on their numbers is negligible.

The leopard seal is the chief predator of Antarctic penguins while they are at sea. This sinister-looking individual (above) surfaced near our Zodiac while we were investigating the stranded group of Adélies (right) that were waiting things out on a jagged bergy bit near Esperanza. Two of the birds, their white breasts drenched crimson with blood, had been badly mauled but were lucky enough to have escaped with their lives. Although leopard seals are basically krill-eaters, those individuals that live near penguin colonies feast largely on penguins and thus, in a sense, get their krill secondhand.

142

Man, the most lethal predator of all, was not a serious menace to penguins until he exploited the Subantarctic islands in recent times.

Huge boilers or "digesters" (above) on Macquarie Island bear silent witness to the slaughter of penguins that took place during the last century. Today, they rust away in the sea wind while the Royal Penguins find a sanctuary on this southernmost "green" island.

CHAPTER 6
Trials and Tribulations

A penguin is by no means the silly, carefree bird that its appearance and demeanor might suggest. Nor is its life a comedy. Rather, as Louis Halle puts it in *The Sea and the Ice*, "It is . . . like the tragedy of Canio the clown, whose role it is to get slapped, his face frozen in its comical expression as he plays his part out to its fatal end."

Consider the Adélie, braving the bitter winter gales at the edge of the Antarctic ice pack, eluding the jaws of the leopard seal, walking perhaps as much as 50 or 60 miles over the sea ice to reach its nesting site when the austral spring impels it to reproduce its kind, and then facing the ruthless competition and in-fighting of the colony. Always there is the overriding urgency of finding enough krill to sustain life.

In this chapter, I shall not dwell on the storms, the search for food, or the other environmental factors that make a penguin's life so rigorous, but tell about their predators, which, in a very definite sense, includes man.

Leopard seal

$\mathbf{T}$he leopard seal, sinuous and serpentine, is the principal sea-based predator of penguins in the Antarctic, and therefore the popular concept is that this marine mammal eats little else. This is not so. It is not a herd animal as are most of the other pinnipeds, except on rare occasions. It is a loner. Yet there are far more of its kind than we would have guessed. Some recent estimates would put the world population of leopard seals at 300,000 or more. Considering that each penguin colony is patrolled by only a very few of these seals, a diet of penguins cannot account for the bulk of the population.

As many as 18 Adélies have been found in the stomach of a single leopard seal. But assuming that each one ate only two penguins a day (which would probably be a starvation diet), the yearly toll of penguins would be in excess of 200 million. It is very doubtful that there are that many penguins in the Antarctic. Obviously, most leopard seals also eat other items—fish, squid, young seals, and so forth. I recently learned from a biologist of the British Antarctic Survey that leopard seals are basically krill-eaters and that only those whose territories are adjacent to penguin colonies live largely on penguins. In a sense, they get their krill preprocessed.

Penguins are well aware of the leopard seal. They recognize that threatening prowler at a considerable distance. The outsized head, long ragged mouth, and flexible neck give it an aspect quite unlike that of any other seal, but to prudent penguins, any dark floating object that looks remotely like a seal's head, even an empty oil can, is suspect. If they are not sure the coast is clear, they cannot be forced to enter the water. A photographer bent on getting action pictures will have to wait. If he presses them, they will double back and even dodge between his legs.

I have watched leopard seals intercepting Adélie Penguins not only at Cape Crozier, but also at Cape Adare, Cape Bird, Cape Hallett, Cape Royds, Hope Bay (or, as it is more properly called, Esperanza), and a dozen other places. I also have witnessed their attacks on Chinstraps at Deception Island and at Elephant Island. The technique is always the same. A penguin is seized in the great wide mouth and thrashed about on the surface of the water like a dishrag until it is literally peeled out of its skin. Bits and pieces float away, and eventually the ragged pelt or skeleton is washed up on the beach, where the skuas and sheathbills pick off any fragments of flesh that remain. Usually, the intact head is attached to the skeleton; this is characteristic of a leopard seal kill.

I have often wondered whether inexperienced young birds are more vulnerable than the more experienced adults. I suspect they are. The adults certainly know what a leopard seal is. It is indelibly printed on the limited penguin mind, and when that distinctive head appears, even in the distance, they discuss things excitedly. There is a babble that plainly means "leopard seal." Penguins coming in from the sea are in a frantic hurry to jump ashore or to seek refuge on a handy ice floe. Those penguins that had intended to leave the colony for the fishing grounds gang up by the hundreds on the rocks or along the ice lip and wait until the menace is gone, no matter how long it takes.

At Cape Crozier, when brash ice impeded the incoming Adélies, I watched leopard seals catch them with ease. I suspect that in ice-free water the birds can outswim their pursuers, or at least put on the burst of speed that may mean survival. When about to make a landing, they come in fast, sometimes porpoising, sometimes zigzagging just below the surface. Reaching shore, they pop out like jack-in-the-boxes or as my wife put it, "like slippery watermelon seeds," landing upright on their feet or sometimes on their bellies. If there has been an error in judgment or if the landing platform of ice or rock is too high (more than four or five feet), they may plop back into the water to make another try. It is at this

Adélie Penguins

awkward moment that incoming birds are most vulnerable to the leopard seal lurking beneath the ice lip.

I suspect (but have no proof) that leopard seals may employ a kind of sonar to gauge the thickness of ice and to pinpoint objects, such as penguins, on it. At Cape Crozier, as I listened to the eerie sounds that emanated from the floes under which a leopard seal was patroling, this occurred to me. I was struck by the tactics the animal used in trying to seize a lone Adélie, probably an inexperienced youngster one or two years old, as it tried to come in over the newly formed ice. The sinister-looking head of the leopard seal suddenly emerged, sending the penguin racing away in panic. The seal submerged, and a moment or two later broke through the thin crust within two or three feet of the terrified penguin which again scampered a short distance and stood still with flippers quivering, hardly knowing where its pursuer might surface next. After three or four near misses by the seal, the distraught bird gained the land. Several other Adélies, whose skeletons, heads still attached, washed ashore to be picked clean by the skuas, were not so lucky.

One afternoon at Esperanza, on our way back to the ship, we came upon 60 or 70 Adélies that had been pinned down on a small berg or bergy bit by a leopard seal. The huge sluglike seal, ten feet long, could be seen in the plankton-turbid depths as it cruised beneath our Zodiac. Surfacing occasionally, its head above the green water, it looked us over, eyeball to eyeball.

Two of the birds on the ragged islet of ice had breasts drenched with blood and flippers torn. Badly mauled, they had somehow escaped to join the others on the ice. They would probably survive. Not so lucky was an incautious individual that plunged in (or did it slip?) and tried to make it to shore. In a flash, the leopard seal had it. Grasping it by the head and thrashing it this way and that, the seal quickly killed it while its terrorized companions watched.

Leopard seals find easy pickings on the outer rim of Deception Island, that extraordinary volcanic island where whalers formerly sought harbor. Here, where there is a huge colony of Chinstraps, it is not ice that makes landing difficult but the surf that beats incessantly against the lower ledges, sending great fountains of spray into the air. Incoming penguins are often washed from the rocks back into the sea. One afternoon I watched a single leopard seal take or injure half a dozen Chinstraps in an hour. One poor bird escaped twice while it was being mauled about, only to be grabbed a third time, still struggling. It hardly seemed fair; it was a sloppy operation on the part of the seal.

In the stormy waters around South Georgia, leopard seals are the most important sea-based predators of King Penguins. Around the Antarctic continent, even the remains of Emperor Penguins have been found in the seals' stomachs.

The leopard seal is not the only seal that will grab a penguin given a chance. There is a definite predator-prey interaction between most of the southern "eared" seals and penguins; New Zealand fur-seals have been known to take Erect-crested, Royal, and Snares Penguins; the South African fur-seal preys on Jackass Penguins; Hooker's sea lions sometimes take Yellow-eyed Penguins and Gentoos; and southern sea lions are quite capable of catching Magellanic Penguins, Gentoos, and Rockhoppers. Apparently, the practice is widespread among the otaridae.

Fur seals

Kelp gull

The kelp (or Dominican) gull, the southernmost representative of the black-backed gull complex, eats penguin eggs when it gets a chance, and it is perhaps for this reason that the Magellanic Penguin finds it advantageous to keep its eggs out of sight if it can—in a burrow or under a bush. However, a gull would be badly lacerated if it pressed its luck; no other penguin has a nastier bite.

The smaller dolphin gull, grayish with a bright red bill and red feet, is an even more aggressive egg-snatcher, but is more local in its distribution. It lives only around the southern tip of South America and in the Falklands.

The most efficient avian predator of all is the skua, a relative of the gulls, a dark hawklike bird with large white wing flashes. In the Adélie colonies of Antarctica, it takes not only eggs and chicks but also adults if they are weak, sick, or injured. This bird, like most scoundrels (if I may be anthropomorphic), is very resourceful. Two or more skuas may work as a team, one diverting the penguin's attention from its eggs while the other quickly darts in and snatches one of them. Or two or three skuas may badger the "aunties" guarding a crèche until one of the youngsters breaks away and is snatched aloft or is bowled over and pecked to death.

Some visitors to the Antarctic who are biologically naive may take the view that penguins are "cute little fellows" that must be protected from the hungry aggressive skuas. Such self-appointed guardians have been known to shoot skuas, even though it is illegal to do so. Skuas must live too—and so must leopard seals. When either of these predators manages to get a penguin—and it is not easy—they are working within the natural system, a mutually beneficial economy that has evolved over the millenia. There is a limit to the number of individuals of any species, be it penguin, seal, or man, that an ecosystem will support. Thus, there is constant interaction, and by means of natural selection, things are kept somewhat

Giant fulmar

The giant fulmar, with a seven-foot spread of wing, may at times kill many penguin chicks and even adult penguins, a sight I have witnessed at Macquarie Island, where some birds have developed the technique of standing in midstream and intercepting Royal Penguins as they file up or down the shallow streambed that leads from one of the large colonies to the sea. The pressure of the numbers of birds simultaneously going up or down the narrow confines of this watery corridor hemmed in by walls of poa grass and Macquarie cabbage makes it almost impossible for individual penguins to escape this rather ugly, rapacious predator, which normally scavenges the sea. The streambed is lined with the bones of penguins picked clean by giant fulmars and skuas.

A group of French scientists studying the Emperor Penguins at Pointe Geologie reported that one-third of the mortality of chicks was due to giant fulmars. Similarly, the most important avian predator of the King Penguin also is the giant fulmar. It is most likely to cull out the weak or injured chicks and sometimes a very sick adult; therefore, like some other predators, it tones up the health of the population.

Killer whales, so numerous along the edge of the Ross Ice Shelf and elsewhere about the rim of Antarctica, also take Emperor Penguins on occasion, but it is not known how frequently they add these large divers to their diet.

Blizzards and foul weather are greater hazards to these ponderous penguins. When Edward Wilson investigated the Emperors at Cape Crozier during the Scott expeditions of 1902 and 1911, he noted a very high mortality of eggs and chicks, both years, due apparently to unstable ice conditions, which kept many parents from feeding their chicks. The little things became emaciated and eventually froze to death. On the basis of these two expeditions, one could have deduced that either Emperor Penguins had the longevity of humans (70 years or more) or else were a vanishing species. Neither conclusion is correct. Today, we know that those two years recorded by Wilson were not typical. There are years, however, when there may even be a total wipeout of reproduction. This may happen when the sea ice breaks loose from the Ross Ice Shelf prematurely during a storm, and the half-grown young are carried to their destruction.

A rare and most unusual predator, the striated caracara, or "Johnny Rook," pressures the Rockhopper Penguins in the Falkland Islands. Lars Lindblad and I watched two or three of these raiders as they grabbed fluffy young Rockhoppers from the midst of the colony on West Point Island. Predation such as this would seem costly to Rockhoppers because they never rear more than a single chick even though they lay two eggs. But considering the immense numbers of Rockhoppers, the toll taken by caracaras is negligible.

"Johnny Rook"

An Adélie Penguin's life on the Antarctic continent is structured in a rather simple way. There basically is only one sea-based predator, the leopard seal, and in most colonies only one aerial or land-based predator, the skua. By contrast, the Galápagos Penguin, small in numbers and living close to the Equator, has a much more complex set of predation pressures.

On islands such as Isabela, where cats and dogs now run wild, Galápagos Penguins and their chicks are vulnerable to these introduced mammals. The scarlet crab, often called "Sally Lightfoot," that swarms over the rocks attacks weak or abandoned chicks. The endemic Galápagos rat and the introduced Norway rat also eat eggs and young birds. Even the Galápagos hawk has been recorded as a predator on penguin chicks. At sea, it is quite likely that the Galápagos fur seal and the sea lion, as well as sharks, may catch the adults. Tuna fishermen take them alive at times in spite of legal protection.

The smallest and northernmost penguins on the other side

Scarlet crab

of the Pacific, the Blue and the White-flippered penguins of Australia and New Zealand, also are beset by many hazards and pressures. At sea, they must contend with fur seals and sharks as well as skuas and large gulls. Ashore, they are victimized by introduced animals such as dogs, foxes, cats, rats, ferrets, and stoats. Their remains have even been found in or under the nests of white-breasted sea eagles. Tiger snakes enter their burrows to devour eggs or chicks, and, probably, large lizards do the same. While still in the nest, some young succumb miserably to attacks by swarming fleas and ticks.

In Chapter 2, I touched on the impact that Europeans had on penguins when they first met. Ships' diaries reveal the large numbers that were taken to insure the survival of the crews. One Elizabethan explorer, Captain John Davies, killed and dried 14,000 Magellanic Penguins. A Dutch navigator, Van Noort, took 50,000 to provision his expedition. For 300 years, ships of Spain, Portugal, England, Holland, and other countries took their toll.

This killing for food could be condoned more readily than the commercial slaughter that took place at Macquarie, South Georgia, the Falklands, and other Subantarctic islands during the 1800s, when penguins of several species were boiled down *by the millions* for their oil.

It was not so many years ago that some penguin colonies were exploited for leather goods, particularly in Argentina. However, these days in much of South America, as elsewhere, it has become unthinkable to kill or harm the *pajaro nino*, "child bird."

Man, in his burgeoning numbers, has affected the fortunes of penguins in varying ways. Dr. William Sladen had calculated that the available krill that would have been eaten by baleen whales had they not been killed off by the whaling

156

industry is sufficient to support at least 300 million more penguins. Obviously, there has been no such population explosion, but there is evidence that those krill-eaters that live on the fringe of the Antarctic, the Chinstrap, the Adélie, and to a lesser extent the Gentoo, have increased markedly, especially in the vicinity of the Scotia Arc and South Georgia, where whalers formerly were most active.

Those penguins that were subject to direct persecution for their oil also are showing increases—especially the handsome King Penguin. The colonies of Kings in South Georgia are larger than they were a few years ago, and the one at Macquarie Island is making a strong comeback. During my visits to that southernmost green island near the Antarctic convergence over a period of ten years, I have noted a dramatic increase, especially at the northern end of the island, where nonbreeders and immatures gather to loaf on the beaches.

On the debit side, two species have shown decreases that, if they continue, could put them on the endangered species list. The Peruvian Penguin declined drastically because the deep beds of guano in which it digs its nesting burrows have been stripped away for commercial phosphate fertilizer.

On the other side of the world, its counterpart, the Jackass Penguin, living on the islands of southwest Africa, dropped from a population of millions early in the present century to an estimated 250,000 by 1956 (Rand). The latest estimates put the figure somewhere between 100,000 and 160,000. Whereas commercial egging caused most of the decline, crude oil spilled into the sea by tankers is now the greatest threat.

It may seem incongruous that in this motor age penguins may even be killed by cars—as sometimes happens when Little Blue Penguins in Australia and New Zealand walk at night from the sea to their burrows. At one colony of Magellanic Penguins at Cabo Virgines on the Strait of Magellan, I have seen dozens of dead birds where a motor track crosses their colony.

When a site for a new Antarctic station is chosen, it is often near a penguin colony. This is understandable; a good spot for penguins to come ashore is also a good beach for landing craft. This can be unfortunate for the penguins as at Hallett, Cape Royds, Esperanza, Gonzalez Videla, and a number of other stations.

Built in 1957, Hallett Station forced the immediate dispossession of 7850 Adélies, which were fenced from their breeding grounds. Thousands more were displaced as buildings and installations were erected within the rookery. The accumulated trash, which became a vexing problem, continued to encroach on the colony. Even some of the scientific work had a detrimental effect. Thus, the nesting pairs of Adélies at Cape Hallett declined markedly. Skuas also suffered a high mortality. They were killed by misguided station personnel who observed them eating penguin eggs and chicks. It is sometimes difficult to explain convincingly the predator-prey relationship to well-meaning people who are biologically illiterate. Recently, there have been plans to move the station, and some of the mess has already been cleaned up. This is all being done in the hope that the penguins will repopulate their former area.

The VIPs from McMurdo who simply wanted to see penguins visited the relatively small colony near Shackleton's hut at Cape Royds so often that the colony declined to a point where restrictions had to be imposed. Actually, there are some very good provisions in the Antarctic Treaty aimed at safeguarding penguins: vehicles may not go near colonies nor can explosives be used near them; helicopters are forbidden to fly over or to make landings closer than 300 meters.

Although these rules exist, I have seen them violated at times, as when a helicopter flew low over the Adélie colony at Cape Royds, panicking many of the birds.

Sledge dogs must be kept chained; penguins have no fear of them. On the Fildes Peninsula, where a Russian and a Chilean base have been built within a few hundred yards of each other, a pet husky belonging to the Chileans was allowed the liberty of the beaches, where it annihilated many of the Chinstrap Penguins when they came ashore. The Russians were upset about this, so to protect their own good relations with their neighbors, the base commander asked me, an American, to intercede with the Chileans about the dog. "We don't like what is happening to the penguins, but we have to live with these other fellows, you know," he explained. My mission was delicate, but it succeeded. The next year, when I returned, the dog was gone and penguins again had safety on the beach.

The Antarctic avifauna evolved on a continent that knew no land-based mammalian predators—neither man nor wolf—until the first explorers arrived with their sledge dogs. The husky is of the same ancestral heritage as the wolf, and left to its own devices reverts to a wolf's ways. It can play havoc with penguins. At Esperanza, I was distressed to see huskies tethered in a long line directly in the path of many home coming Adélies. After landing on the beach, the birds had to walk a quarter of a mile over the snow to the sprawling rookeries on the slopes behind the station. Any penguin that passed through the line of dogs was chopped to bits. The snow was covered with blood, and we saw several birds that managed to get through the gauntlet alive, but with a leg or a flipper torn off. We were told that some days earlier a husky broke away from its traces and made a beeline for the Adélie colony, where it killed 50 birds before it could be caught. It is quite possible that escaped huskies could establish themselves as Antarctica's wolf packs, surviving on a diet of penguins and seals.

Tourism now has reached Antarctica. On expeditions in which I have participated, we have always briefed the passengers before going ashore, requesting them to respect the environment and the rights of wildlife. We urge them not to walk through a penguin colony but to observe it from the perimeter.

Nearly all the breaches of ecoconduct that I have witnessed in Antarctica have been not by tourists but by station personnel. Attitudes vary. At stations where biologists are working, the rules may be strictly observed. At others, more technologically oriented, they may be ignored. But even biologists, if not scrupulously careful, can disrupt the penguin colonies they are studying.

With the recent awareness that an ecological crisis of global proportions is developing, environmentalists are taking a closer look at the Antarctic. They have found DDT and other chlorinated hydrocarbons present in the fatty tissues of Adélie Penguins. How did these biocides reach the shores of the Antarctic—by ocean currents, by air, or through the food chain? Their presence confirms the dictum of the National Audubon Society that "DDT anywhere is DDT everywhere."

To repeat a thought I expressed earlier: Penguins are an indicator of the health of our watery planet, and if they are unable to survive, we had better take notice or we might find our own survival threatened.

CHAPTER 7

The Neighbors

On the open sea, a penguin surfaces as an albatross sweeps by. They share the same oceanic environment and compete in very different ways for much of the same food supply—fish, squid, and krill.

Neighbors at sea, they also may be neighbors ashore in some of the places where they nest, such as Elsehul in South Georgia. On this steep-sided fiord, thousands of Macaroni Penguins swarm over the rocky talus, jostling, jabbing, shoving, and yelling, each pair disputing two or three square feet of space with other Macaronis.

Ignoring their rowdy relatives (which branched off the same family tree long ago), a scattering of black-browed albatrosses, *Diomedea melanophris,* sit serene and silent. Each incubating female squats atop a foot-high pedestal of mud, upon which rests a single large chalky egg. They occupy sites on promontories around the rim of the colony, where they can readily land or take off into the wind. The hordes of penguins, on the other hand, must make it on foot from the landing beaches, as we must, struggling up little rocky paths through the deep tussock grass.

As we watch the show, several male black-brows glide by, hanging momentarily on the updrafts as though to check if all is well at the nest. Or one of them may settle down beside its mate. This is invariably followed by a ritual of strutting, bowing, tail spreading, mutual nibbling, and preening, all calculated to keep the pair-bond strong.

The black-browed albatross or mollymauk, which superficially resembles an oversized black-backed gull, and the much larger wandering albatross, *D. exulans,* which has a white back, are the two species of albatrosses that follow ships most persistently. Hundreds of nesting black-brows dot some of the precipitous slopes at Elsehul, but the wandering albatross prefers the flatter moors of Bird Island off the western tip of South Georgia.

On the steep sides of Elsehul at the edge of the Macaroni colony, single pairs of light-mantled sooty albatrosses, *Phoebetria palpebrata,* also have taken up residence. They are loath to leave their nests as we try to climb past, and if we extend a hand toward them, they nibble our fingers reprovingly. This species is the most elegant of all the albatrosses; in flight, its pointed tail gives it a more streamlined look, and its slim wings are more sharply angled. It is the most maneuverable sailplane of them all; the wilder the gale, the better it flies.

Farther along the hillside, in a little suburb of their own, are a few gray-headed albatrosses, *D. chrysostoma,* rather like the black-brows but with smoky gray heads and black-and-yellow bills. They do not follow ships as habitually as the black-brows and therefore are not as familiar to the birdwatcher at ship's rail. They too are completely tame, for like most other albatrosses they evolved in a part of the world where men and their predacious ways were unknown until relatively recent times.

Black-browed albatrosses share colonies with Macaroni Penguins.

Albatrosses are the largest flying seabirds. They have the longest and narrowest wings, which on the wandering and the royal albatross, *D. epomophora*, may exceed 11 feet. Although they may rest buoyantly on the sea, they cannot take off unless lifted by the wind. To become airborne, they must flap laboriously and paddle along the surface with their huge webbed feet. Once free of the waves, their flight seems effortless; they are masters of dynamic gliding. They take advantage of the layer cake of wind that is at full strength approximately 50 feet above the water and is progressively slowed by friction closer to the surface of the sea. The bird glides downwind on stiff wings until it nearly touches the waves; then it makes a wide swing into the wind. Lifted by layers of wind of ever-increasing strength, it climbs to the 50-foot level again, swings downwind, and repeats the pattern, which may resemble a great figure eight. In this manner, it exploits the air currents effortlessly for hours at a time.

Most of the squid and fish are probably caught at night because, watch as we might during the day, we do not see albatrosses snatch them from the water. They keep on gliding, wheeling, and gliding endlessly. However, the wandering albatross, the black-brow, and one or two of the other mollymauks have learned to scavenge refuse thrown from the ship's galley, and like the giant fulmars and other ship-followers, they settle in the wake when such goodies are available.

Albatrosses live a long time; with luck, a wandering albatross may survive 50 years or more. They are slow to mature and may not breed until the ninth or tenth year; in contrast to this, Adélie Penguins breed in their fourth year, King Penguins in their fifth or sixth. Because albatrosses enjoy such long lives and are so relatively free of predators, a single egg at each nesting is enough to insure a stable population; indeed, the wandering albatross and the royal albatross lay but one egg every second year.

All of the albatrosses in the Southern Hemisphere— nine species—associate with penguins at some time or other, either casually at sea or more intimately in a few mixed or adjacent colonies. On the other hand, the three albatrosses that are confined to the North Pacific never make contact with penguins.

The other large ship-follower, the giant fulmar, *Macronectes giganteus*, sort of a "poor man's albatross," is not as benign in its relationship with penguins. At Esperanza on the Antarctic Peninsula, I have watched one harass a large crèche of young Adélies while a single adult penguin successfully defended them. At Macquarie Island, giant fulmars habitually intercept Royal Penguins as they parade down to the sea in a small stream from the colony back of Nuggets Point.

Giant fulmars come in a variety of shades, from very dark through intermediate shades to pure white. The incidence of whiteness increases as you move southward toward the Antarctic continent. Some giant fulmars are more immaculate than the whitest wandering albatross.

Many sites where penguins have established their colonies are shared not only by albatrosses but also by shearwaters, petrels, and storm petrels that nest in burrows in the turf or in crevices in the rock. Because of their nocturnal and subterranean habits, these lesser tube-nosed seabirds often are overlooked. On a night visit to a colony of Little Blue Penguins on Phillip Island near Melbourne, Australia, I found that more than half of the burrows were occupied by short-tailed shearwaters ("mutton birds"), *Puffinus tenuirostris*, dark petrels that make long migrations throughout the Pacific Ocean.

Wilson's storm petrel

"Muttonbird"

In colonies of Chinstrap Penguins during the half-light of the polar evening, I have watched Wilson's storm petrels, *Oceanites oceanicus,* fluttering into their nests under the boulders, while on the cliffs above, cape pigeons, *Daption capensis,* sat stolidly on their eggs. These two species frequently followed the ship, and we looked for them from the stern as they wove a criss cross pattern in our wake. Penguins, on the other hand, usually are seen from the bow as they porpoise away when our ship overtakes them.

The ocean is so featureless that one would expect not only specialists such as penguins, which live their lives as avian submarines, and albatrosses, which spend their days gliding, but also generalists—standardized birds that can do most anything in the marine environment. The gulls are, in fact, the median-line of seabirds.

Gulls are the ultimate compromise for the oceanic environment. Their flight is leisurely; their legs are strong for perching on rocks and for walking the beaches. They can glide, maneuver quickly, hover in one spot, and make pinpoint landings. They cannot dive from the air as well as terns or gannets, glide quite as efficiently as albatrosses or petrels, soar as effortlessly as frigatebirds, or swim as vigorously as ducks. However, with more or less competence, they can do all of these things.

The most widespread of all the gulls in the far South is the kelp gull, *Larus dominicanus,* which some authors prefer to call the southern black-back. It is very much like the familiar great black-backed gull of the North Atlantic except for its greenish instead of flesh-colored legs. An older name was Dominican gull, an obvious reference to its bicolored "habit."

The kelp gull may take the eggs and chicks of other seabirds when it has a chance. Actually, there is somewhat of a trade-

Antarctic tern

Arctic tern

off; the attrition of its own eggs and chicks to skuas and other gulls is believed to be close to 50 percent. At Punta Tombo, I once watched a kelp gull leave its nest momentarily to chase off a sheathbill. While its back was turned a dolphin gull, *Leucophaeus scoresbii,* a smaller and more aggressive species, moved in, snatched an egg, and broke it.

Of all the winged predators, the skuas, *Catharacta,* heavily built gull-like birds, that are strong and uncompromising, are the ones most intimately associated with penguins. In Chapter 6, I have described their predator-prey relationship—the teamwork of skuas and the penguins' defense. In a very real sense, skuas have helped to make penguins the tough birds they are.

Although skuas and gulls may sometimes give penguins a rough time, taking their eggs or small chicks, the smaller, more graceful terns tend to ignore penguins unless one happens to walk too close to their nests; then they may dive-bomb it, swooping with angry cries, urging the trespasser to move on.

The Antarctic tern, *Sterna vittata,* is the prevalent "sea swallow" of the Southern Ocean. Like many other terns, it is pearly gray and white with a red bill and a deeply forked tail. On King George Island in the South Shetlands, at the edge of a mixed colony of Adélie, Chinstrap, and Gentoo Penguins, I know a busy ternery. Here the birds lay their eggs high on a massive rock that juts from the sea where there is no danger of being trampled by penguins.

During the austral summer, the terns in the Antarctic may be joined by Arctic terns, *Sterna paradisaea,* the greatest travelers of all. When these migrants are present in the polar seas of the Southern Hemisphere, they may be known from the resident terns by the white foreheads of their nonbreeding plumage. They may associate with auks during the northern summer, then leave long before the freeze to consort with penguins in the corresponding latitudes of the far South. In so doing, they enjoy more hours of daylight during the course of a year than any other birds in the world.

The more northerly penguins may share the sea briefly with migrating Arctic terns, but they are more likely to come in daily contact with other kinds of terns. The Peruvian Penguin in its sea caves on the guano islands consorts with the most bizarre species of all, the Inca tern, *Larosterna inca,* a blackish bird with a scarlet bill and flowing white mustaches.

Inca tern

A visitor to a colony of Adélies or Chinstraps in the American sector of the Antarctic might mistake the sheathbills, *Chionis alba,* for white pigeons. This is understandable. Or he even might take them to be ptarmigan as did some Norwegian sealers who tried to eat them, much to their regret. However, no pigeon or ptarmigan would pick the eyes out of a newly hatched baby penguin if it were left unguarded. A sheathbill would do so without hesitation.

Sheathbills can be a nuisance to the penguins, but basically, they are scavengers, cleaning up krill or fish that have been dropped, eggs that have been abandoned, or anything else edible that is lying about. Therefore, it is not surprising to find them searching for tidbits at sewer outlets in the Fuegian towns of Ushuaia and Rio Grande or at rubbish heaps at stations around the Antarctic Peninsula.

Cormorants or shags of at least 15 kinds share the colder sea currents of the Southern Hemisphere with penguins. Only one, the blue-eyed shag, *Phalacrocorax atriceps,* crosses the convergence to the Antarctic Peninsula. Its eyes are really brown; the broad rings around them are blue. When standing

Blue-eyed shags share some colonies with Gentoos.

erect on the rocks, a blue-eyed shag, with its formal black-and-white attire, may look rather like a penguin except for its longer neck and thinner bill, but the illusion is shattered when it takes wing.

At Port Lockroy on the Antarctic Peninsula, I repeatedly have visited a mixed colony of blue-eyed shags and Gentoo Penguins, which at a distance appears to be all penguins. The shags have their own enclave on a little bluff, where they can launch into the wind. The penguins step away from their eggs or chicks momentarily when I use the wide-angle lens on them at minimum range, but the shags do not budge; they shake their open bills threateningly and glare at me through blue spectacles.

Cormorants swim low in the water, as penguins do, but their long slim necks are held erect, not pulled in to the shoulders. They do not porpoise. They get sodden rather quickly, so they do not spend too much time swimming; after fishing a bit, they take off for the rocks along the shore, where they stand upright and half spread their wings to dry the flight feathers.

Wherever penguins live, seals of one sort or another also are to be found. I can think of no exceptions. They forage in the same seas, and sometimes one must look carefully when small fur seals are porpoising to make sure that they are not penguins. Although the leopard seal is the only seal that habitually feasts on penguins, any of the eared seals (sea lions and fur seals) might take penguins on occasion. In the Antarctic, one often sees lines of Adélies walking by within two or three feet of the noses of sleeping Weddell seals and on the ice floes they frequently consort with crab-eater seals. Except for the leopard seal, the true seals pose no problems; but even the leopard seal is no threat when it is ashore.

The seals around many of the Subantarctic islands have made a strong comeback since sealing was stopped, and nowhere is this more evident than at Elsehul in South Georgia. When one looks down from the bluff at the head of the bay, the vista below is a scene of confusion. Bull fur seals rush about among the tussock grass, defending their harems from their rivals; pods of molting elephant seals sprawl indolently on the beach like gargantuan slugs, while little parties of King Penguins and Gentoos wander aimlessly among them. The Gentoos in the large colony on the saddle above the beach are finding access increasingly difficult. Because of the explosive growth of the fur seal population, they soon may be dispossessed.

King Penguins are not intimidated by fur seals.

Although elephant seals often lie in their wallows very close to the muddy rookeries of King Penguins, they are, I suspect, kept out of the nurseries by the vicious jabs of dozens of irate birds. I have not actually observed this, but I cannot account otherwise for the fact that the blubbery animals do not create havoc. I know that a King Penguin refuses to be intimidated by a fur seal; it stands its ground and makes a threatening gesture if the animal does not move off.

Did penguins—and fur seals—learn about "porpoising" from the masters themselves, by imitation? Or is the habit just another example of convergent evolution—totally unrelated animals doing the same thing because they share the same environment and a similar way of life? In the oceans of the Southern Hemisphere there are many kinds of porpoises, or dolphins, some of them strikingly patterned. Perhaps the most beautiful is Commerson's dolphin, which is largely white with black markings. One can count on seeing it in the Strait of Magellan not far from Isla Magdalena, where the Magellanic Penguins have their historic colony.

King shag, a Patagonian neighbor of the Magellanic Penguin

At Punta Tombo, a two-mile-long finger of land on the Patagonian coast, the swarms of Magellanic Penguins live in rather close association (although not always in harmony) with at least 20 other species of birds. The tip of the peninsula is dominated by cormorants of three species, mostly king shags, *P. albiventer,* and rock shags, *P. magellanicus,* but there also are a few pairs of guanays, *P. bougainvillii.* This is the only nesting spot on the Atlantic side of South America for this Peruvian species—the guano-producing cormorant. On the open sandy ridges, terns of at least three species as well as dolphin gulls concentrate in dense colonies. More scattered are the kelp gulls and brown skuas. The gulls and the skuas are potential predators on the eggs and chicks of penguins, but they seem to find easier pickings in the cormorant colony. The cormorants are a bit more casual about guarding their offspring and probably cannot inflict the serious damage on a gull or a skua that a penguin can with its razor-sharp mandibles.

On the rocky back side of the peninsula, where few penguin-watchers venture, I chanced upon the large stick nests of a dozen pairs of egrets, *Casmerodius alba.* I was hardly prepared to find a heronry in the midst of a penguin colony, particularly with so many egg-hungry kelp gulls about.

Even rheas (South American "ostriches") and guanacos (relatives of the llama) roamed the point, while along the outer shore, where the penguins congregate in vast numbers, there were steamer ducks, *Tachyeres;* Oystercatchers, *Haematopus,* of two species; and little parties of sheathbills.

Farther south on the Patagonian coast, at Rio Deseado, Magellanic Penguins breed in close association with neotropic (olivaceous) cormorants, *P. olivaceus.* The cormorants build their nests on the tops of the bushes, the penguins in burrows beneath. Here I found the most unusual penguin's nest in all my experience. It was three feet from the ground in an abandoned cormorant's nest. Some of the sticks in the old structure had slipped off to the side, forming a ramp up which the innovative pair of penguins could climb.

On the coasts of Patagonia and particularly the Falklands, penguins often associate with the gooselike birds known as

sheld geese. The most marine of these is the kelp goose, *Chloephaga hybrida*, a dimorphic species whose dark females are almost invisible as they swim among the greasy ribbons of giant kelp, quite in contrast to the white males, which can be spotted half a mile away. On New Island in the Falklands these geese stroll about the slippery ledges of the Rockhopper colony, while long lines of penguins file by, intent on their own busy errands.

Even the more abundant upland or Magellan geese, *C. picta*, may leave the moors in the Falklands for the edges of the sea after the young have hatched, and I have seen so many parents with their broods in the surf and along the shore that the Gentoo Penguins literally had to shove their way through the crowd to get to their colony back in the meadow. The homecoming Gentoos hastened across green lawns dotted with goose droppings where Falkland thrushes, *Turdus falcklandii*, resembling washed-out American robins, hunted for worms.

Ducks are no strangers to penguins. In the Falklands and in Patagonia, I often have seen steamer ducks and crested ducks, *Anas specularoides*, swimming among Magellanic Penguins. In a rocky cave in the Aucklands, south of New Zealand, at a place where Yellow-eyed Penguins come ashore, I spotted a pair of the very rare Auckland teal, *Anas auklandica*. The small flightless ducks were almost invisible as they made their way through the dense beds of giant kelp. I made a similar discovery at the edge of a large King Penguin colony at the Bay of Isles in South Georgia. From the tussock grass almost under my feet scampered two small brown ducks with yellow bills. They were South Georgia pintail, *Anas georgica*. Unlike the secretive teal of the Aucklands they can fly, but seem reluctant to.

It is to be expected that the Jackass Penguin of South Africa would have a different set of neighbors. Cherry Kearton, an early British bird photographer, recounting his experiences on Dassen Island near Cape Town more than 50 years ago, stated unequivocally that there were millions of penguins on that island. Today, only a small fraction remains, and I shall explain in Chapter 9 some of the reasons for this drastic drop in numbers.

Steamer ducks swim among Magellanic Penguins in the Falklands.

Even in his day, Kearton was under the impression that the penguins were declining. He laid much of this to their "enemies"—the kelp gulls and sacred ibises, *Threskiornis aethiopicus*, that snatched unguarded eggs and chicks, the lurking octopus that waylaid birds entering or returning from the sea, and the sharks that swarmed around the reef biting off the legs of penguins that managed to escape. Of course, the penguins had always lived with these hazards, and it was not until man added his pressures that the balance was badly tipped against them.

When writing about penguins, Kearton was unabashedly anthropomorphic, so it followed that if penguins had "enemies," they also had "friends." Among these he included the cape gannets, *Morus capensis*, that lived in a great colony nearby; the black oystercatchers, *Haematopus moquini*; the various plovers, *Charadrius*, that often shared the exposed reefs with the penguins; and the lumbering tortoises that sometimes toppled clumsily into the nesting burrows.

The runty-looking penguin of the Galápagos has perhaps the most varied collection of associates of any penguin in the world. On Fernandina, I have seen a penguin surrounded by large scarlet crabs as it preened itself on the dark lava. I watched another standing quite unconcerned in the midst of an assemblage of marine iguanas, looking as unreal as a gnome surrounded by dragons.

The penguins show no apparent interest in the scarlet crabs nor in the marine iguanas, but the herons do. The yellow-crowned night herons, *Nyctanassa violacea*, that stalk among the rocks include crabs in their diet, and the great blue herons, *Ardea herodias*, often take young iguanas. The small dark lava herons, *Butorides sundevalli*, prefer tiny fish that they catch in the shallow tidepools. Even though these various

Cape gannets live with Jackass Penguins in South Africa.

herons inhabit the same rocky coves where the penguins haul ashore, there seems to be no real competition.

Tropical seabirds, such as brown pelicans, *Pelecanus occidentalis*, blue-footed boobies, *Sula nebouxii*, and brown noddies, *Anous stolidus*, also fish in Galápagos waters, but their assault is from above, whereas the penguins pursue their prey underwater. There also are two endemic gulls that nest only in the Galápagos, the lava gull, *Larus fuliginosus*, a smoky-colored bird that may number only 400 pairs, and the more numerous and very beautiful swallow-tailed gull, *Creagrus furcatus*.

Of all the marine birds that the Galápagos Penguin meets on the black rocks of Fernandina and Isabela, none is stranger than the flightless cormorant, *Nannopterum harrisi*.

When a flightless cormorant plunges beneath the water, it uses its broad webbed feet for propulsion, not its wings; the tatty, nonfunctional wings are pressed close to its body, while it speeds on its submarine quest for squid and fish. At Point Espinosa, I once saw one surface with its face enveloped in the writhing tentacles of a small octopus that it had caught.

(Previous spread) On a South Georgia beach near Grytviken, an immature King Penguin mingles with elephant seal pups.

Royal Penguins consort with elephant seals on a Macquarie Island beach. The sham fights of the "unemployed" young bulls do not seem to alarm the hordes of penguins, but earlier in the season, when the big beachmasters fight, the contests can be frightening and bloody. Whereas other seals and sea lions may sometimes pose a danger to penguins, the big lumbering elephant seals do not.

179

Pinnipeds of one sort or another are found around virtually all of the islands where penguins live. Even in the Galápagos, sea lions and fur seals are present and, given the opportunity, might take penguins as most other eared seals do. The leopard seal is not the only seal that relishes their flesh.

The penguin-watcher on the hauling grounds of sea lions and fur seals must be alert. I have been chased by belligerent bulls and even truculent cows on the beaches of Enderby, at Point Espinosa in the Galápagos, and at Elsehul in South Georgia, where I encountered the formidable fur seal above. I was busily concentrating on Gentoo Penguins when this whiskered face showed itself above the poa grass and forced me to take my investigations elsewhere.

A gray-headed albatross wheels in for a landing at Elsehul in South Georgia. On these headlands, this species as well as three other kinds of albatrosses, the black-browed, the light-mantled sooty, and the wandering make their homes, while nearby are noisy colonies of Macaroni, Gentoo, and King Penguins. Now that South Georgia is no longer a shore base for the whalers, key breeding places like Elsehul are unmolested and, in effect, have become sanctuaries.

At Punta Tombo in Patagonia, where more than 1 million Magellanic Penguins raise their families, they associate freely with at least a dozen other species of aquatic birds.

In this photograph, which I exposed in the cormorant colony at the tip of the point, I have managed to show several king shags on their nests, while three other species of birds await a golden opportunity to steal a momentarily unguarded egg. The large gull with a blackish back is a kelp gull; the smaller grayish gulls are dolphin gulls; and the white dovelike birds are sheathbills. The shags are more vulnerable to these egg-snatchers than are their neighbors, the penguins, which lay their eggs in shallow burrows or under bushes where they at least have minimum protection.

One day, I saw a fox wandering among the penguin warrens. This resourceful animal would seem to have easy pickings, but Magellanic Penguins are not chickens. Their razor-sharp bills demand respect.

184

A royal albatross, incubating its egg, surveys a breath-taking vista on Campbell Island. Five species of albatrosses and three of penguins make this Subantarctic island south of New Zealand their natal home.

Gliding on the sea wind, the albatross lives an aerial existence that no penguin can experience. Yet evolutionists believe that penguins are more closely related to these master gliders and their smaller kin, the petrels, than they are to any other birds. They are presumed to have had a common ancestor, but during the process of adaptive radiation by natural selection, the penguins branched off the main line and lost the power of flight, while the albatrosses refined the technique of avian gliding to its supreme expression.

185

A kelp gull (left) takes off from its icy perch. Ranging farther south than any other gull, it lives close to many penguin colonies, where it may take unguarded eggs, but basically, it makes its living by scavenging the tidelines and the sea.

At first glance, blue-eyed shags (below) might suggest thin-necked penguins, but the illusion is shattered when they take wing. They share living space with Gentoo Penguins at Port Lockroy on the Antarctic Peninsula, where we landed from the Explorer the day before Christmas to have a Swedish "glögg party" and to share the holiday spirit with the birds.

The penguins' look-alikes in the northern oceans are the auks and their kin, such as the murres (above) and the puffins (right). Although they are unrelated to penguins, they fill a similar niche. Like the penguins, auks stand erect on land and use their wings underwater, whereas most other diving birds employ their webbed feet to propel themselves when swimming below the surface. However, except for the great auk, which is now extinct, auks have not lost the ability to fly.

The two species of murres (called guillemots in Britain) are the most widespread of the auk family, inhabiting both the Atlantic and Pacific oceans. Some colonies on the sea cliffs of the north rival in size the largest penguin rookeries.

Puffins (right), with their rotund bodies and great colorful bills are attractively grotesque. Confined to the North Atlantic, this species finds its greatest abundance in Iceland. Two other species of puffins live in the North Pacific and in the Bering Sea.

Two razorbills (below) jostle for a position on a North Atlantic island. Whereas penguins, living in a terrain devoid of land mammals, do not need to fly, their northern counterparts, such auks as the razorbill, must often contend with foxes and other land-based predators. For them, flight is essential to reach the safety of ledges on cliff faces, where four-footed animals cannot go.

Auks face a greater hazard at sea, where bilge oil dumped from ships may gum up their plumage. It is suspected that the recent decline of razorbills in many colonies in the North Atlantic is due primarily to oil slicks.

Crested auklets (above) cluster penguinlike on the boulders of St. Lawrence Island in the Bering Sea. When my plane descended to the Gambell airfield, I could clearly see Siberia, only 50 miles away. A young Eskimo who actually owned a copy of my Field Guide to Western Birds *took me to the cliffs where the auklets swarmed. The compact flocks, as well-drilled as starlings, flew in from the sea, almost brushed the cliff face, flew along it, and swung out over the water again. Crouching low, I waited until a flock settled a few feet away, then took this picture. At close range, with their forward-curling topknots and grotesque smiles on their waxy bills, the strange noisy auklets looked too absurd to be true. In the foreground of the group is a least auklet, the smallest seabird of the Bering Sea.*

population that had been all but wiped out by a volcanic eruption in 1830. The last great auk in Scottish waters was killed in 1840 on Stac-an-Armin by a St. Kildan who thought it was a bogie. The species had already ceased to exist on the western side of the Atlantic, where a large colony had once flourished on Funk Island off Newfoundland.

In spite of visual similarities, the great auk and its lesser relatives (which include the auks, auklets, murres, murrelets, guillemots, and puffins) are quite unrelated to the penguins. Penguins belong to an order of their own—*Sphenisciformes*—and it is thought that they share a common ancestry with the petrels and albatrosses. On the other hand, the auks are related to the gulls, terns, sandpipers, and plovers. These rather disparate families are placed together in the order *Charadriiformes*.

Unrelated though they may be, the auks replace the penguins ecologically in the northern oceans. No auks have ever been recorded in the Southern Hemisphere. And no penguins penetrate the Northern Hemisphere, except for those few Galápagos Penguins that barely slip across the Equator on Isabela Island.

Aside from their black-and-white patterns and erect postures, auks and penguins have another thing in common. When traveling underwater, they use their wings for propulsion as though they were flying. With the exception of the diving petrels, all other submarine swimmers primarily use their webbed feet.

The great auk was the only one of its family to lose the power of flight. All living members of the clan can fly. A good thing, too, because unlike the Antarctic, the Arctic has a number of land-based mammal predators. Only by nesting on cliffs can most colonial birds be safe from foxes and other

Razorbill

marauders, and to reach those high ledges, a bird must be able to fly.

Great auks were able to waddle ashore and breed in safety on a few rather flat islands, such as Funk, until seafaring men found them. They quite certainly evolved from ancestors that could take to the air, but in their remote sea-girt sanctuaries, there was no need to fly.

The fossil record in the Pliocene deposits of California reveals that once there were flightless auklike birds in the Pacific. They apparently became extinct more than 2 million years ago for reasons that we can never know. Avian paleontologists have placed the two known species in a separate family, *Mancallidae,* the Lucas auks. Although smaller than the great auk, their wings were even more flipperlike.

Great auk

Murres, thick-billed and common

The auk family reaches its most varied expression in the North Pacific and the Bering Sea, and may have originated there. Of the twenty-one living species, only six reside in the Atlantic and of these, three (the dovekie, razorbill, and Atlantic puffin) are confined to that ocean; the other three (the two murres and the black guillemot) range across to the Pacific side as well.

The teeming colonies of murres (or guillemots as they are known in Britain) are very suggestive of the vast aggregations of penguins in the Southern Ocean, the main difference being one of plane or dimension; their nurseries are usually vertical rather than horizontal. There are exceptions. I had my first preview of what a penguin colony must be like in July 1953, when I set foot in a murre colony on Walrus Island, a rather flat, seldom visited outlier of the Pribilofs in the Bering Sea.

A welcoming committee of Steller's sea lions swam out to meet our dory when we attempted to land on this low rocky island, and the water literally boiled as the big bulls threw themselves off the rocks. But the real show was put on by the murres—the most penguinlike of all the auks. They stood erect, their white shirt fronts contrasting with their dark backs. As we advanced, a solid mass of birds receded before us. Acre upon acre of black-and-white bodies reluctantly gave way and closed in again after we had passed. Each bird guarded a pear-shaped greenish egg and jostled its neighbors for one square foot of space. The density was double that of an Adélie colony, but unlike a penguin colony, the air above was a blizzard of wings.

In 1940, when Dr. Ira Gabrielson visited Walrus Island, he stated that the most conservative estimate ran into the millions. My companions and I were a bit more precise. We made a few sample density counts, then took the detailed charts of the island, plotted the occupied acreage, and arrived at a figure of about 1 million. A lot of birds.

I have visited a great many murre colonies in Canada, Alaska, Greenland, Iceland, the British Isles, and Norway, and all except the one on Walrus Island have been on the ledges of sea cliffs, almost invulnerable to intrusion. If the pyriform or pear-shaped egg is nudged accidentally, it rotates around its small end; it does not roll off the ledge.

The two murres, the common murre, *Uria aalge* and the thick-billed murre, *Uria lomvia*, enjoy by far the widest distribution of all the auk family. There are millions in the polar basin, mostly thick-bills, and their legions range southward in the Atlantic to the Gulf of St. Lawrence and Portugal and in the Pacific to the coastal islands off central California and Japan. The common murre is the dominant species southward.

Leslie Tuck of Newfoundland, who devoted years of research to the murres, estimates a total population of some 56 million, with the thick-billed murre predominating three to one. He says, "I do not think the world population can be less than 50 million. I do not think it exceeds 100 million."

Darwin once wrote that he believed the northern fulmar, a gull-like petrel, to be the most numerous bird in the world. James Fisher, who many years later wrote the definitive monograph on that seabird, disagreed. He stated: "I would be surprised if it [the world population] were as much as two millions and would eat my hat, if I had one, if it were ten millions." The thick-billed murre (with a population of some 40 million) is obviously much more numerous, and Leslie Tuck believes that it may well be the most abundant seabird in the Northern Hemisphere, probably exceeded in the North Atlantic only by the dovekie and in the North Pacific by the least auklet.

Razorbill The great auk's closest living relative, the razorbill, *Alca torda,* is similar in size and appearance to the murres, but its bill is deep and flattened, crossed midway by a conspicuous white mark. It is confined to the North Atlantic, where its numbers are small compared to those of the murres, which are circumpolar. Inasmuch as it winters in the shipping lanes, its ranks have been much thinned by oil spills in recent years.

Of all the auk family, puffins come closest to eliciting the feeling of endearment so often extended to penguins. Because of their clownlike masks and curious waddling walk, they are called "cute" and "adorable." Although the murres are really more penguinlike, most people do not know what a murre is; on the other hand, they often have seen puffins in paintings and photographs.

A puffin is more rotund than a murre or a penguin; it does not stand quite as erect. Its main distinction is its large flat triangular bill, which is gaudily painted with red, yellow, and blue. In winter, it sheds the horny outer sheath like a false nose, revealing a smaller, less colorful bill.

198

Ronald Lockley, the British seabird authority, once estimated the world population of the Atlantic puffin, *Fratercula arctica,* to be about 15 million, of which the greatest percentage live in Iceland. James Fisher was of the opinion that there were between 1 million and 3 million on the Scottish island of St. Kilda alone, but it soon became evident that a crash had occurred. By 1971, when J. J. M. Flegg completed his survey of the Atlantic puffins on St. Kilda, millions of burrows were unoccupied, and only about 163,000 were still active. It was suggested that climatic changes may have affected the food supplies or that oil spills at sea had decimated them as they had the razorbills.

Atlantic puffin

A few puffins nest as far south as Matinicus Rock in Maine. They also bred formerly on Eastern Egg Rock, an island off Muscongus Bay, Maine. In June 1976, when we dedicated this sanctuary to the memory of Allan Cruickshank, the photographer-ornithologist, I was shown a number of hand-dug burrows that would soon be occupied by young puffins flown from Newfoundland. Later that summer, these were hand-fed by several dedicated young people under the direction of Stephen Kress of the National Audubon Society, in the hope that they would be "imprinted" and return as adults to breed on Eastern Egg. As of 1978, several had returned but had not nested.

Unlike the murres, which lay their greenish eggs on bare ledges, puffins deposit their immaculate eggs in burrows they excavate in the turf. For this reason, it is difficult to assess how many puffins live on an island. One cannot scan the cliffs and count them one by one. Most of them may be out of sight in their burrows or at sea, fishing.

The black guillemot, *Cepphus grylle*, a black teal-sized auk with a pointed bill, scarlet feet, and large white shoulder patches, can be found along most of the rocky coastlines from Maine and northern Britain (where it is called "tystie"), north to the Arctic islands. Its colonies are small; scattered pairs nest in crevices among the boulders, often not far above the tide line. There is no mass effect; single individuals sit here and there on the rocks. They frequently whistle weakly in an unauklike manner, revealing a bright vermillion gape.

The similar pigeon guillemot, *Cepphus columba*, of the Pacific coast of North America and the quite dissimilar sooty guillemot, *Cepphus carbo*, of Japan are usually regarded as separate species, but some authorities would lump them with the black guillemot of the Atlantic. They undoubtedly evolved from the same ancestor, which lived in the circumpolar seas.

Pigeon guillemot

The smallest and most abundant of the six Atlantic auks is the starling-sized dovekie, *Alle alle*, or little auk, *Plautus alle*. The population around Scoresby Sound in eastern Greenland has been estimated at no less than 5 million, but that is only a small fraction of the numbers that swarm the coastal screes

Dovekie

of northwestern Greenland. Millions more live in Spitsbergen, Norway, and Novaya Zemlya, U.S.S.R. It is certainly the most abundant seabird of the North Atlantic, to be matched in the North Pacific only by its counterpart, the even smaller least auklet.

They are birds of the drift ice, swimming in the clearings and leads between the ice floes, where they dive for small planktonic crustaceans. They swarm in the icy seas of the High Arctic in incredible numbers. While on an Arctic cruise off Greenland, I watched their great flocks rise from the water like swarms of mosquitoes and drift away like smoke.

Dovekies are widespread in Baffin Bay, ranging literally from one side to the other, wherever there is drift ice; yet inexplicably, they do not nest in the Canadian Arctic (except possibly in one locality). They swarm to Greenland's shores, where they lay their single pale bluish eggs under rocks in the rough screes below the sea cliffs. Enriched by the excreta of countless generations of birds, broad, deep carpets of moss and peat have developed at the foot of the screes. Almost invariably, glaucous gulls nest adjacent to these colonies and feed extensively on dovekies during the summer as do the Arctic foxes. The polar Eskimos also take their share, capturing them by the thousands in long-handled dip nets.

In winter, the frozen sea forces the bulk of the dovekies southward to open water. Some may travel as far south as the English Channel, Long Island, and New Jersey; occasional stragglers reach the Mediterranean and Florida.

Gales at sea sometimes force them landward by the thousands; in an effort to keep offshore, they fight the wind until their fat reserves are exhausted, and scores may be picked up dead or dying along the beaches. After one such "wreck," I found a dovekie swimming in a flooded gutter in Boston.

Tufted puffin

Horned puffin

It is in the Bering Sea that we witness the most varied display of auks. On St. Paul in the Pribilofs, I have seen seven species lined up on the cliffs; every nook and every ledge along miles of rock wall were occupied by murres, puffins, and auklets. James Fisher and I tried to count the murres along a hundred yards of cliff and using this sample came up with a tentative estimate of more than 1 million birds on St. Paul.

Two species of puffins competed for our attention on these cliffs. The tufted puffin, *Lunda cirrhata*, which I had met previously in Oregon and Washington, allowed me to get slow-motion flight shots with my 16mm movie camera as they flew by into the wind. At close quarters on the rocks, they looked too absurd to be real as they turned their huge orange beaks from side to side to see me better. They had outsize orange feet and glorious blond locks that swept back around their ears.

I had expected the other species, the horned puffin, *Fratercula corniculata,* to be rather like the familiar Atlantic puffin, but it had a much yellower bill and, of course, the peculiar erectile horn above each eye. It nested far back in the rocks; the tufted puffin nested in the turf.

Sitting by themselves in pairs or in groups of four to eight were small white-breasted birds with upturned red bills. These were parakeet auklets, *Cyclorrhynchus psittacula*, which are widespread in the Bering Sea and the Aleutians. They nested deep in the crevices from which came their vibrating trills. When I eased up to them on the cliff edge with my Bell and Howell bristling with lenses, I was able to approach within a few feet. Curious about the apparition that confronted them, they resisted the temptation to fly. They nervously stared at me with one white eye, then the other.

Flying by in little flocks as well coordinated as starlings were birds similar in size to the parakeet auklets, but uniform slatey in color. These were crested auklets, *Aethia cristatella*. After they settled on the ledges, I was able to examine their forward-curling head plumes and smiling waxy red bills, which are said to have the odor of tangerines. When I first heard their loud honking, yapping, and grunting sounds under the rocks, I thought I was hearing foxes, with which the island abounds. Like the parakeet auklets, the crested auklets range from the Aleutians through the Bering Sea to northeastern Siberia.

Crested auklet

The midgets of the lot, only six inches long, were the least auklets, *Aethia pusilla*. Buzzing in from the sea like vast swarms of bees, they settled like confetti over the rocks. They sounded more like passerine birds than seabirds, chittering, chirping, and chattering as they went about their business. The Aleuts, who call these stubby little birds "choochkies," catch them in long-handled nets in much the same manner that the Greenlanders catch dovekies.

When James Fisher and I visited the Pribilofs in 1953, we debated whether the murres or the choochkies were the most numerous. Approaching St. George Island in the Fish and Wildlife Service's ship (inexplicably named the *Penguin*), we were staggered by the traffic pouring out to sea from the great cliff of Starya Artil. At least 1 million birds—murres, auklets,

Least auklet, or "choochkie"

203

and puffins—were in sight at one time. Enormous numbers of choochkies swarmed on the rocky hillsides above the town, where they maneuvered like dense clouds of starlings.

Some years ago, one of the men stationed on St. George estimated 36 million choochkies. Fisher and I did not get the impression of such astronomical numbers, nor did Professor Joseph Hickey who recently conducted a survey. But on an earlier visit, Ira Gabrielson had confirmed that there were indeed millions. He commented that the endless processions of sooty shearwaters on the Oregon coast, the blackbird clouds of the Mississippi Valley, and the myriad waterfowl on some of their concentration areas were the only spectacles in his experience that even remotely compared with the auklet hosts of St. George.

Whiskered auklet

More than 100 years ago, when Henry W. Elliot visited the Pribilofs to study the fur seal and bird situation for the U.S. government, he found that the Aleuts had their own names for each of the auks. He recorded *arrie* (murre), *tawpawkie* (tufted puffin), *epatka* (horned puffin), *baillie brushkie* (parakeet auklet), *canooski* (crested auklet), and *choochkie* (least auklet).

The whiskered auklet, *Aethia pygmaea*, in contrast to most of the other auks whose populations run into astronomical figures, is perhaps the rarest of the family. Certainly, it is the least known; its home islands, far out on the Aleutian chain, seldom are visited. This small gray auklet, scarcely larger than a choochkie, is ridiculously ornamented with long white facial plumes.

The rhinoceros auklet, *Cerorhinca monocerata*, the size of a puffin, wears an erect horn on its thick yellowish bill. Although it summers along the North Pacific coast from southeastern Alaska to Washington, it is not well known because

204

of its nocturnal way of life. We seldom see it when it is at sea; it moves into its nesting burrows on spruce or brush-clad islands under cover of darkness.

I once visited a colony on Destruction Island, four miles out in the gray Pacific off the misty Olympic Peninsula. Here these secretive birds were nesting in crannies under a rank growth of ferns, salmonberry, and salal. At sundown, small flocks of them gathered on the water a quarter of a mile offshore, but it was night-dark before they flew in. Not a sound did they make, just a sudden *whir-r-r* and a flutter as they crashed into the bushes and scrambled to their nesting grottoes. All about me, the queer gnomes were fluttering and flapping without uttering a sound. In the light of my flashlight, it was an eerie elfin world.

Rhinoceros auklet

Some of the smaller auks are quite aberrant, almost mysterious. None more so than the marbled murrelet, *Brachyramphus marmoratus,* which lacks the black-and-white pattern of most other auks; instead, it is cryptically barred with dark brown. This should have given ornithologists a hint that its way of life was quite different. Indeed, it was the last North American bird to reveal its nest.

The summer range of the marbled murrelet coincides closely with the damp conifer forests along the coast from southeastern Alaska to central California. This should have given another clue, particularly because the birds' sharp *keer keer* was often heard at dusk or at dawn high over the redwoods.

Although the nest remained a mystery, a fledgeling was picked up on the forest floor 25 miles from the coast of Oregon. Another was found floating down a mountain creek in northern California, several miles from the sea. It was assumed that the nests of this species would probably be found in holes

Marbled murrelet

Cassin's auklet

among the moss and rocks in these foggy forests. It was as much a mystery as "Bigfoot," the legendary anthropoid reputed to range these same forests.

Actually, there was some evidence of tree-nesting. In 1953, two men felled a large hemlock on Graham Island. When they removed the debris, they found a dazed murrelet and bloody eggshells. It could not be determined whether the nest had been in the tree or on the ground where the tree fell. Several years later, in 1967, it was reported that two young murrelets dropped from a cedar felled by loggers three miles from the sea on northern Vancouver Island. Ornithologists generally overlooked the fact that in 1961 the Russians had discovered a nest of the Siberian race of this bird 20 feet up in a larch near Okhotsk.

In 1970, the editors of *Audubon Field Notes* offered one hundred dollars for a picture and proof of an actual nest in North America. Although no one claimed this reward, the first satisfactorily documented nest was discovered on August 7, 1974. Hoyt Foster, a tree surgeon, was trimming branches from a Douglas fir about six miles from the sea in the Santa Cruz Mountains of California. Foster had climbed to a partially dead limb nearly 150 feet above the ground to remove it as a safety precaution to protect a campsite below. On the branch, nestled in the moss not far from the trunk, was a marbled murrelet chick, tan with blackish spots around the face and chest. A mystery that had intrigued ornithologists for 185 years had been solved.

A similar but grayer species, the Kittlitz's murrelet, *Brachyramphus brevirostris*, replaces the marbled murrelet along the coast of Alaska from Glacier Bay north to Point Barrow. It too is somewhat of a mystery, but the scanty evidence indicates that it lays its single olive egg on the bare rocks. One was flushed from its egg in the mountains near Pavloff Bay.

One of the most abundant, widespread—and the plainest—

of the many Pacific alcids is Cassin's auklet, *Ptychoramphus aleuticis,* an obscure gray little seabird with a light spot on its bill. Its colonies, some of them very large, are scattered from the Aleutians to Baja California. Their metropolis on the Farallons off San Francisco was once estimated by William L. Dawson to number 200,000 birds.

Xantus' murrelet

One member of the family, the Xantus' murrelet, *Brachyramphus hypoleucus,* which looks something like an oversized dovekie, ranges south to Cape San Lucas in Mexico. This most tropical of the *Alcidae* lives within 2000 miles of the most tropical of the *Spheniscidae,* the Galápagos Penguin.

I once spent a memorable night in a colony of these small seabirds on the north island of the Coronados off Baja California, twenty-five miles from San Diego. As I lay in my sleeping bag listening to the black storm petrels, *Oceanodroma melania,* that were flitting by like large moths, I heard another voice offshore, a twittering that sounded vaguely goldfinchlike. Taking my flashlight, I threw its bright beam in the direction of the puzzling sounds. I could discern a shape bobbing on the smooth sea. The shape turned into a little bird, black above and white below, which got brighter as it swam closer, like a contrasting print in a developer bath. Dazed by the light, it swam directly toward me, dived, came up again, and reaching the beach clambered right into my waiting hands.

Like the black storm petrel, Xantus' murrelet breeds in crevices in the talus. The babies, born with feet nearly the size of their parents', take to the water when they are scarcely two days old. In contrast, young puffins may spend seven weeks in the nest burrow before leaving for the sea.

Ancient murrelet

Another auk that shares the precocious habit of leaving for the sea when it is only a day or two old is the ancient murrelet, *Synthliboramphus antiquus,* a gray-backed bird with a black face and white eyebrow stripe. Its domain extends from the

Aleutians to the Queen Charlotte Islands in Canada and to northern Japan. The nocturnal exodus of the young was described in 1915 by Professor Harold Heath, who watched it several times with the aid of a lantern. At approximately midnight, the parents commenced a chorus of chirping like house sparrows: "In response, the young, beautiful black and white creatures, as active as young quails, soon poured in a living flood down the hillsides—falling over roots, scrambling through the brush, sprawling headlong over rocks. . . . The surf was pounding violently on rocky beaches, and many times one could see the young swept off the cliffs."

It is evident that the auks, some of which remind us so strongly of penguins, exhibit every bit as much diversity in their breeding biology and their way of life as their look-alike counterparts in the Southern Hemisphere.

Black guillemot

CHAPTER 9

Interacting with Men

Penguins coexisted with aboriginal men for centuries around the southern extremities of the continents. The relationship may have been an uneasy one for the birds, but the penguin nations in their millions were not really threatened until men from the Northern Hemisphere arrived. The impact was lethal.

The early European explorers and the adventurers who followed held the egocentric view that these plump birds were put in these remote latitudes by divine providence to insure their survival. Whole fleets were provisioned with them as I noted in Chapter 2.

During the four and a half centuries since da Gama and Magellan, penguins were slaughtered for their flesh, their oil, and their skins; they were used for bait; their eggs were taken from them. Introduced animals preyed on them and eroded their nesting habitat, pollution befouled their seas, and lately the food supplies of some species have been drastically reduced by the fishing fleets. Directly or indirectly, untold millions of penguins have been destroyed by men.

The history of the Subantarctic and cold-temperate islands is a conservation shocker. Many of them were raped beyond redemption. When the Falkland Islands were first settled, it was standard practice to set fire to entire islands to get rid of the jungles of tussock grass, and large numbers of penguins perished in the flames.

Although penguins always had been considered fair game in the Falklands, it was not until the middle of the nineteenth century that they were heavily commercialized; hundreds of thousands were slaughtered annually for their oil, which had many uses in those days. The little Rockhoppers took the brunt of the carnage. A single Rockhopper rendered a pint of oil, a Gentoo somewhat more. In 1857, four small schooners in the Falklands "tried out" 50,700 gallons of penguin oil, implying a take of more than 400,000 penguins in a single season. Ian Strange, the Falkland naturalist, calculates conservatively that during the years when this was going on as many as 2.5 million birds were killed.

During this extractive period, no penguins were more vulnerable than the big stately King Penguins. Their dense colonies were on flat exposed terrain where they could be herded together and clubbed to death. It has been said (but it may be apocryphal) that the last colony in the Falklands was destroyed by a shepherd for the sole purpose of oiling his roof.

King Penguins survived in South Georgia even though the elephant seal hunters took them in large numbers along with the more abundant Gentoo and Macaroni Penguins. Their oil was used to top off barrels of seal oil, and their skins were fed to the fires under the trypots in which seal blubber was rendered down. For these purposes, 500,000 to 700,000 penguins were sacrificed annually.

210

When the sealers first came to Macquarie Island, south of Australia in the 1820s, King Penguins were massed in two immense colonies. The Lusitania Bay colony was so large that as many as 60,000 birds could be seen entering or leaving the sea at any hour. After the hundreds of thousands of fur seals had been exterminated and the elephant seals were reduced to a remnant, the sealers turned their attention to the Kings as a source of oil. When these gentle birds had dwindled to an unprofitable few, the Royal Penguins were next. Somehow, through sheer numbers, they survived the annual toll of 150,000 birds, mostly the young of the year, until public opinion in Australia forced an end to the industry.

A trio of Kings

Rockhopper Penguin

In several island communities in the South Atlantic, the gathering of penguin eggs became traditional. On Dassen Island near Cape Town, eggs of Jackass Penguins were gathered by the hundreds of thousands annually under government sponsorship until it became evident that the huge colony had diminished by 90 percent. At remote Tristan da Cunha, Rockhopper eggs still are gathered when the islanders make their pilgrimages to nearby Nightingale Island.

In the Falklands, several thriving colonies were decimated or wiped out by egging. A colony of Rockhoppers at Sparrow Cove near Stanley yielded 25,000 eggs in 1871. None are there today. Until recently, the schoolchildren in the Falklands were granted a holiday, around November 9 (coinciding with Lord Mayor's Day in England), to go egging and to have a picnic.

The assault on penguins involved even their tough durable skins, which were made into caps and all manner of clothing, including footwear. King Penguins furnished the largest and most beautiful pelts. The yellow plumes of Rockhoppers were fashioned into table mats and other ornaments by the beauty-starved homesteaders of lonely Tristan.

Penguin skin was quite popular for leather goods, and until quite recently, I could still find billfolds made of penguin leather in the shops of Buenos Aires. In the mid-1950s, a dealer in that city was granted a government permit to take 30,000 Magellanic Penguins from the colony at Rio Deseado in Patagonia. This would have wiped out the entire colony if George Casares, the grand old man of Argentine bird protection, had not heard about it in time to have the permit revoked.

Today, conservationists worry about only three of the world's 17 species. The others seem to be quite safe; they enjoy stable populations. The three that bear watching all belong to the Harlequin or Jackass group. They are the African Jackass, the Peruvian, and the Galápagos Penguins. The fourth member of the genus *Spheniscus*, the Magellanic Penguin, far outnumbers its three cogeners combined and seems to be prospering in nearly all of its many colonies along the coasts of Patagonia, Tierra del Fuego, and the Falklands.

The Galápagos Penguin routinely appears on lists of "endangered species" and is almost certainly the penguin with the smallest population. Its numbers have been variously estimated at 1000 to 5000, but may be closer to 15,000 as the recent investigations of Dee Boersma suggest. There is no evidence that its numbers are diminishing as are those of its close relatives the Jackass and Peruvian Penguins. Its future lies in the stability or lack of stability of the Cromwell Current.

As recently as thirty years ago, live Galápagos Penguins brought by fishing boats to the docks of San Diego could be purchased for as little as twenty-five dollars. On the other hand, Adélie Penguins, swarming by the millions in the relatively inaccessible Antarctic, were unavailable at any price. The Galápagos Penguin is now protected by Ecuadorian law, and we no longer hear of it being offered for sale, nor are any being held in captivity by any of the major zoos.

The population of the Galápagos Penguin, although small, is relatively stable, quite unlike that of the flightless cormorant with which it associates. I was told by an Ecuadorian conservation officer that in one year in the late 1960s at least 100 cormorants were drowned in lobster traps put out by Japanese fishing fleets. The penguins, feeding at lesser depths, escaped these traps.

The Jackass Penguin of Africa, the first penguin known to Europeans, is in deepening trouble. Pycraft stated in 1906 that there were 9 million on Dassen Island. Kearton, who was there during the 1920s, put it at 5 million, and he challenged anyone to prove there were fewer. Both certainly were overestimates; an informed guess, based on old photographs, apparent densities, and the size of the island, is that there may have been 1.5 million. Today, less than 65,000 remain.

It is now believed that this catastrophic decline was due largely to commercial egging. Between 1917 and 1927, as many as 500,000 eggs were removed from Dassen every year. After 1927, the annual harvest dropped to 400,000, then to 170,000. By 1949, it was down to 97,000; in 1964, 57,000. As late as 1967, one could still order penguin's eggs in the restaurants of Cape Town, but in 1968, all egging was stopped. By then, other pressures were building up. The South African inshore fishing industry and fishing fleets from other nations were making deep inroads into the declining stocks of pilchards and anchovies. Penguins were almost certainly feeling the pinch.

But an even greater threat is oil. As early as 1952, mortality was noted among the seabirds because of oil spills around the cape. The hazard remained negligible until 1967, when the Suez Canal was closed, and oil tankers were forced to go around the Cape of Good Hope. Today, 750 tankers a month, one for every hour of each day, pass close by Cape Town. A great many are new supertankers, which would not be able to negotiate the Suez. There have already been several major tanker disasters, releasing black tides of oil onto the cape seas. In April 1968, when the *Esso Essex* struck a submerged object, she spilt 4000 tons of oil. About 1700 oiled penguins were picked up. Inasmuch as it is calculated that eight to eleven birds perish at sea for every oiled bird that makes it to the beach, this single disaster caused the deaths of 14,000

Baby Jackass Penguin

to 19,000 penguins. Another tanker accident, also in 1968, destroyed 8000 penguins on Dyer Island, the entire population.

Many oiled birds are salvaged by compassionate people in Cape Town who endeavor to clean them and save their lives. A voluntary organization, the South African National Foundation for the Conservation of Coastal Birds, has taken on this task. Some penguins liked their treatment so much that they returned to Cape Town after their release.

The combination of commercialized egging, overfishing, and chronic oil pollution has reduced the African Jackass Penguin to perhaps 10 percent (some say 4 percent) of its former members.

Although the plight of the African species has been much publicized, I suspect that its Peruvian counterpart is even more endangered. I know of no colony of any large size today. The reason for the drastic decline of the Peruvian Penguin is unique in the annals of wildlife conservation; as previously noted, its nesting grounds were literally dug up and shipped to the ends of the earth. Formerly, the penguins dug their burrows in the dense layers of guano—the dried excreta of cormorants, boobies, and other seabirds—that had accumulated since time immemorial in this arid climate. Ancient eggs exhumed from the deep beds of fossil guano dated back thousands, if not tens of thousands, of years. As late as the middle of the last century, many islands, in the words of Robert Cushman Murphy, still "had their crusts as full of penguins as a cheddar is full of skippers."

The ancient Incas knew all about guano and its value as a fertilizer—it was many times more potent than ordinary manure—and so did their Spanish conquerers. Small vessels were laden with the precious substance to enrich the fields of Peru. The resource seemed inexhaustible.

Jackass Penguin

By the middle of the nineteenth century the fame of this miraculous fertilizer had spread to the United States and to Europe, and so great was the demand for it throughout the world that in 1860, 433 vessels loaded at the Chinchas. Millions of dollars, amounting to three-fifths of the total public revenue, poured into the treasury of Peru.

When the fossil guano, which at its greatest depth had measured 180 feet, was excavated down to bare rock, the guano fleets went elsewhere. Although guano still is harvested, only the yearly deposit is now available; this is seldom more than ankle deep, not deep enough for a penguin to burrow into. Inevitably, the great populations of penguins along the coast faded away.

Today, the remnants of this once-abundant species find precarious nesting sites in a few places, but even these survivors are threatened. Local fishermen take the eggs and chicks whenever they find them and destroy many adults in their nets. I walked through a fishing village near Paracas and discovered many more penguins dead along the beach than I was to see alive in the nearby waters. I believe that this may be the penguin in the most serious trouble. It is high on the list of priorities of Peruvian conservationists, such as Felipe Benavides.

And yet when Janet Gailey-Phipps, a protégée of Professor William Sladen, recently made a survey of penguins held in captivity, she found that at least 32 zoological parks and aquaria throughout the world exhibited Peruvian Penguins, far more than any other species. Second in number was the Jackass Penguin of Africa, exhibited by 21 institutions. Actually, the latter was represented by the greatest number of individuals (about 270) and enjoyed the greatest breeding success. It is no accident that the greatest numbers of penguins in captivity and those that breed most readily are these two species that inhabit temperate climates.

Until quite recently, the tragedy was that so many penguins, particularly the cold-adapted species, succumbed to heat exhaustion during the long journey by plane or by ship to the Northern Hemisphere, or did not survive after they arrived. Refrigeration or air conditioning minimizes the danger; lacking these facilities, they sometimes are sprayed with a hose or force fed with pieces of ice or snow.

Once settled in their quarters, the birds run the risk of contracting *aspergillosis,* a respiratory disease that is fatal if it is not treated soon enough. Some zoos have lost nearly all of their birds to this ailment.

A third hazard is bacterial infection—E. coli, Staphylococcus, Streptococcus, and so forth; the list is long. Coming from places where they were relatively free from contamination, penguins become highly susceptible in the contrived environment to which they are transferred.

Although the truly Antarctic penguins, such as Emperors and Adélies, must be housed in refrigerated indoor exhibits, others do well in outdoor pools and enclosures. In fact, they are more likely to breed successfully out-of-doors, especially if they have an ample water area, but they run a greater risk of picking up bacterial infection and mosquito-borne viruses, such as bird malaria.

Of the 500 or more important zoos and aquaria throughout the world, perhaps only 50 institutions in a dozen countries maintain exhibits of these popular birds. Today's first-line zoos, with skilled staffs that include dietitians and pathologists, are very sophisticated in their techniques for keeping their charges healthy and happy.

It would seem an anomaly that the two most endangered penguins are the ones most frequently seen in zoos. The question naturally follows: have zoos contributed to their decline? Almost certainly not. A single oil spill off the Cape of Good Hope will wipe out far more Jackass Penguins than have ever

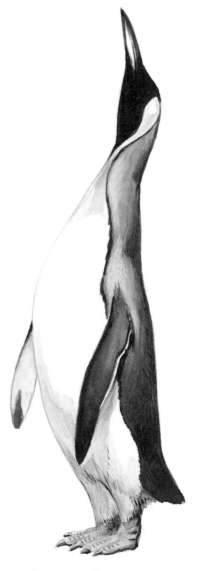

King trumpeting

217

been held in all the zoos of the world. Likewise, a single foray by the anchovy fleet in Peru can result in far more dead penguins than are to be seen alive in all the zoos.

There can be a very positive side to zoological exhibits. They make it possible for people to know animals that they may never have a chance to see in the wild, and they also may act as a holding reservoir for endangered species—*if they can be bred*.

Recently, at a convention of the American Association of Zoological Parks Administrators in Baltimore, I chaired a seminar on penguins in which the many problems of keeping them were discussed—diet, care, pathology, and presentation to the public. At the close of the meeting, we passed a resolution that we hoped would be adopted by all zoological parks and aquaria—that no exhibitor should keep only one or two penguins of a species; if they had singles, they should send them off to zoos that had others of the same species in order to build up viable flocks. It was recommended that no zoo should keep penguins unless they had a minimum of ten of a kind. Because penguins depend on social stimuli, ten was considered the minimum number that would assure successful reproduction.

At the Baltimore Zoo, an outdoor primate exhibit was converted into a penguin colony. The monkeys were banished from their rocky island, which was surrounded by a moat, and 30 Jackass Penguins were put there. The oval channel that isolates their citadel gave the penguins uninterrupted swimming. They also had access to a cavelike chamber in the island in which each pair had its own little nesting house, like a small dog kennel.

When I was admitted to their sanctuary, the guardian angel of the little flock was Janet Gailey-Phipps, mentioned above.

She was studying their community behavior, which has all the variety and aberration of a Peyton Place. She pointed out a bully, an incorrigible Lothario, a homebreaker, and a thief who was forever filching twigs from the nests of its neighbors. One bird was hopelessly frigid, while another showed homosexual tendencies. When one of the penguins sent shock waves through the vaulted room with its asthmatic braying Gailey-Phipps commented: "That's 'Old Blue'; he's the noisiest one." She knew each bird intimately; they did not need name tags.

The Edinburgh Zoo in Scotland has had the longest unbroken history of displaying and breeding penguins. For more than 50 years, King Penguins have reared young in this zoo, and lately, it has distinguished itself by its extraordinary success with Gentoos. In 1974 alone, the number raised was 28, and the total Gentoo flock had increased to 118, emphasizing the fact that penguins need company and that the larger the flock the better their reproduction.

Many years ago at the Edinburgh Zoo, a keeper left open the gate to the penguin enclosure, and when one of the penguins followed him, he conceived the idea of taking his charges for a walk. King Penguins, Gentoos, and others soon lined up at the appointed hour (11 in the morning) for their constitutional, and not only did they walk the pathways of the park but they also were allowed onto the streets of Edinburgh, where they were introduced to the alien world of buses, tramcars, and motorcars. Because of the danger of traffic accidents, this part of the walk was canceled after a few months, and the parade took place within the confines of the park.

Gentoos in a hurry

Australia has its own well-publicized penguin parade. About 50 years ago, after a road was built across Phillip Island near Melbourne, a young bus driver, Bert West, took people to watch the Little Blue Penguins as they came ashore on moonlit nights. He became upset at the way things were going after a bridge from the mainland was built, unleashing a flood of uncontrolled tourists, bathers, and picnickers. They intercepted penguins trying to come ashore at night and frequently ran over them in their cars as the birds tried to get from the beach to their burrows in the scrub-covered dunes.

Things reached a critical state in 1955. On some nights, only a very few of the beleaguered birds got through to their nests. Hundreds of young died of starvation. Bert West pleaded to the State Fisheries and Wildlife Department of Victoria to do something. They took prompt action, setting aside a ten-acre sanctuary in the area known as Summerlands and declaring much of the beach out of bounds to humans between sunset and sunrise.

And yet the show was able to continue, as I witnessed one summer evening. As dusk fell, floodlights were switched on and crowds of onlookers gathered behind two parallel fences to wait for the penguins to plod up the broad corridor of sand that led from the beach to their nesting area, which was guarded by a high wire fence. A voice in the control box gave a few informative comments about penguins, and very shortly, a wave rolled in and receded, leaving a little gaggle of dripping figures on the sand where there had been none a moment before. Another wave rolled in, submerging them momentarily, and when it receded there were twice as many. Their numbers augmented, the little platoon of gleaming blue-black gnomes hurried self-consciously between the rows of spectators to their sanctuary. On some evenings, as many as 5000 people have assembled to watch the show.

Little Blue Penguin

Chinstraps greeting

By and large, the fortunes of penguins, their ups and downs in historic times, have been closely linked with the activities of men. Although the Jackass and Peruvian Penguins are in serious trouble, and the Little Blue and possibly one or two others may have diminished somewhat because of foxes, dogs, cats, and other introduced animals, the populations of most species are quite stable. As has been pointed out, the Chinstrap and the Adélie may actually be increasing because of the overkill of whales; the krill that the whales would have eaten are now available to penguins.

Because of protection, King Penguins are making a strong comeback. Whereas they were once down to a low of perhaps 6000 on Macquarie, there has been a progressive increase. The colonies on South Georgia also are prospering, and a scattered few individuals even have returned to the Falklands, where they now nest in four places.

During the early days of Antarctic exploration, Adélie Penguins were fed to sledge dogs, but today, this is forbidden by the Antarctic Treaty, ratified by 12 governments in 1961.

The present century has seen the rise of a conservation conscience. Except for a few vestiges of traditional exploitation, we are developing a new altruism, if we can call it that. Penguins now enjoy our concern; they are protected. We also have entered an era of science and inquiry.

Paradoxically, the most accessible penguins, those living in temperate latitudes, were long ignored by biologists and behaviorists, while the Adélie Penguin, living remote from civilization on the Antarctic continent, received more attention than all other species combined.

We know about the composition of Adélie colonies; their locations and their magnitude; their population increases and declines; the aging process and mortality, as well as interaction with predators. We have learned much about the food habits of these birds, their swimming and diving, their social behavior and display, communication by body language, communication by voice (determined by tape recordings), and orientation (determined by telemetric devices). Under laboratory conditions, Adélies have been dissected; their skulls and their skeletal structures have been analyzed. Their embryology has been investigated as well as the protein structure of their eggs.

Because of grants and other funds available for polar research, we know much more about the Adélie Penguin that lives in the most remote part of the world than we do about the robins that walk on our lawns.

Only very recently have there been any really critical studies of the Jackass, Magellanic, Galápagos, and Little Blue Penguins. The Peruvian Penguin, perhaps the most endangered species, still awaits investigation. We know very little about its ecology, ethology, and population dynamics, or even its numbers.

Scientific research eventually filters down to the public, and it was inevitable that nature-oriented people would want

222

to see for themselves the Antarctic and its penguins. A few tourists are now yearly visitors to the Antarctic. Tourism of the right sort is a good thing because it bolsters conservation efforts as well as scientific inquiry.

To me, watching penguins has been a moving, thought-provoking experience. Although they may look a bit like little brothers nattily dressed in feathers, they respond to life rhythms quite alien to our own. They are dedicated to being penguins, and they are good at it. Because of their great numbers and the simplified ecosystems in which they live, we can readily observe cause and effect, some of the basic principles of survival—and life.

Magellanic Penguins

Photographic Postscript

There are nearly as many wildlife photographers these days as there are bird watchers, and therefore, the reader of a book such as this, more often than not, is curious about the photographic equipment that was used.

First, let me say that all the photographs in this book, except seven, are mine. The photograph of the swimming Peruvian Penguin, a zoo bird, was taken by Russ Kinne. My own shots from a cliff top in the Chinchas were not good enough to use. The photograph of the Snares Penguin is the work of Lester Peterson, a companion on several expeditions who is, I believe, the only person other than myself who has seen every one of the world's 17 penguins in the wild and who has photographed them all. My own shots of the Snares Penguin, taken from the deck of the ship, were much too distant. George Holton, who also accompanied me on many trips, furnished the shots of the Fiordland and Erect-crested Penguins and the "Johnny Rook." The leopard seal with the

Adélies was taken by Robert Hernandez, and the murres, by Dan Guravich.

The majority of the pictures were taken with my battery of Nikons; a few with my Hasselblads. I prefer the latter for black and whites; the larger format offers greater flexibility when making enlargements.

Three of my Nikons are motorized (one has a sports-finder), useful when shooting flying birds. Penguins are not airborne, except momentarily when plunging into the sea (p. 84) or when porpoising, and it is then that the motorized equipment is indispensable.

The lenses I most often use on the Nikons range from wide-angle to telephoto (28mm, 35mm, 55mm micro, 105mm, 180mm, 80–200mm zoom, 300mm, and 400mm), all in the Nikkor series. Because of their extreme tameness, penguins can often be photographed with the wide-angle 28mm or 35mm lenses. This has the advantage of greater depth of field, encompassing with reasonable sharpness both the close-up penguin and the distant landscape.

In addition to my Nikkor series, I have also used the 400mm Novoflex on a gunstock and also the 640mm extension. This lens is better than it should be considering its reasonable price. I am less enthusiastic about my two mirror or reflex lenses, the 500mm and the 1000mm. They are relatively light and convenient but lack flexibility because of their fixed apertures. They also seem to lack full color saturation. What I dislike most is the feeling of astigmatism or ghost image that one has when details are just beyond critical focus. Of course, because penguins are what they are, I have seldom resorted to long focal lengths when photographing them.

On my Hasselblads, I employ the 80mm and 250mm Carl-Zeiss lenses.

As for flash or fill-in light, I have tried at least a dozen different strobe outfits. Whenever there is a breakthrough or some sort of imagined advantage, I buy a new one. I can offer no useful advice about this. However, penguin photography seldom requires artificial light, but there are gloomy days when it helps.

In my earlier color work, I used Ektachrome and Kodachrome in about equal amounts. However, I experienced far more disappointments and exposure failures with Ektachrome, especially when using High Speed (EH). This may have been due in part to the reaction of my meters to the cold. Today, I favor K64, but use ED 200 when necessary. For black and white, I prefer Panatomic X.

Roger Tory Peterson

February 1979

Further Reading about Penguins

There are a number of books about penguins, including some specifically for young readers. I can think of at least three or four that were written by authors who had never seen a penguin in its home environment. In addition, there are hundreds of articles and papers, ranging from popularly presented to highly technical. In preparing this book, I have consulted scores of such publications, but those listed below are the ones I would most recommend for further reading, either for pleasure or for information.

BOERSMA, P. DEE, "An Ecological and Behavioral Study of the Galápagos Penguin." *The Living Bird*, Fifteenth Annual.
CHERRY-GARRARD, APSLEY, *The Worst Journey in the World*. London, Constable, 1921. A dramatic account of a six-week journey in the polar night to secure eggs of the Emperor Penguin at Cape Crozier.

Ithaca, N.Y., Cornell Laboratory of Ornithology, 1976, pp. 43–93. A very thorough technical account dealing with environmental adaptations of this tropical penguin.

JARVIS, CAROLINE, ed., "Penguins in Captivity," *International Zoo Yearbook*, Vol. 7, section 1. Zoological Society of London, 1967. A symposium by zookeepers on the problems of keeping penguins.

KEARTON, CHERRY, *The Island of Penguins*. London, Longmans, Green, 1930. A rather anthropomorphic but entertaining narrative about a photographer's camp-out among Jackass Penguins on Dassen Island in South Africa.

MURPHY, ROBERT CUSHMAN, *Oceanic Birds of South America*. New York, American Museum of Natural History, 1936. Vol. 1, pp. 329–471. Extensive and scholarly accounts of the penguins of South America but somewhat outdated by more recent studies.

OLNEY, P. J. S., ed., "Penguins," *International Zoo Yearbook*, Vol. 18, section 1. Zoological Society of London, 1978. A symposium (chaired by Roger Tory Peterson in Baltimore) on the problems of keeping penguins in zoos.

PETTINGILL, ELEANOR RICE, *Penguin Summer*. New York, Clarkson Potter, 1960. A well-written story of a summer in the Falkland Islands studying penguins and filming them for Disney Productions.

PETTINGILL, OLIN SEWALL, *Another Penguin Summer*. New York, Scribners, 1975. A photographic sequel to *Penguin Summer*. The Pettingills return to the Falklands and the penguins. Eleanor wrote the previous book, Sewall this one.

PHILIP, MARIE, *Gregory Jackass Penguin*. Cape Town, David Philip, 1971. The story of a pet penguin and the efforts of people in Cape Town to save oiled Jackass Penguins.

RANKIN, NIALL, *Antarctic Isle*. London, Collins, 1951. Wildlife in South Georgia vividly described and photographed by one of the world's finest bird photographers.

RICHDALE, L. E., *Sexual Behavior in Penguins*. Lawrence, Kansas, University of Kansas Press, 1951. For the ethologist.

RICHDALE, L. E., *A Population Study of Penguins*. Oxford, Clarendon Press, 1957. An exhaustive study of the Yellow-eyed Penguin of New Zealand.

ROBERTS, BRIAN, ed., *Edward Wilson's Birds of the Antarctic*. London, Blandford Press, 1967. A fine large book featuring the drawings and paintings of penguins and other Antarctic birds by Wilson, the great naturalist on the Scott expeditions.

SIMPSON, GEORGE GAYLORD, *Penguins: Past and Present, Here and There*. New Haven and London, Yale University Press, 1976. An erudite overall discussion, emphasizing history and prehistory.

SOPER, TONY and SPARKS, JOHN, *Penguins*. England, Newton Abbot, David and Charles, 1967. A general book on penguins with much good information, clearly presented.

STONEHOUSE, BERNARD, *Penguins*. New York, Golden Press, 1968. A popular but authoritative book by a man who has done a great deal of scientific work on penguins. Well illustrated with photographs.

STONEHOUSE, BERNARD, ed., *The Biology of Penguins*. London, MacMillan, 1975. Technical papers and reviews by 27 authors on various aspects of penguin research.

WATSON, GEORGE E., *Birds of the Antarctic and Sub-Antarctic*. Washington, D.C., American Geographical Union, 1975. A field guide with fine capsule summaries of penguin life, history and biology.

YOUNG, PAMELA, *Penguin Summer*. Wellington, N.Z., Reed, 1971. A graphic and amusing account by a biologist's wife of their summer among the Adélies at Cape Bird on Ross Island.

Index

Entries in **boldface** *refer to illustrations.*